# *Whispers from the Lord*

Other books in the Arlene Schuiteman Series

*Sioux Center Sudan: A Missionary Nurse's Journey*

*Iowa Ethiopia: A Missionary Nurse's Journey Continues*

*Zambia Home: A Missionary Nurse Endures*

Additional books by Jeff Barker

*Performing the Plays of the Bible: Seven Ancient Scripts and Our Journey to Return Them to the Stage* (coauthored with Thomas Boogaart)

*The Storytelling Church: Adventures in Reclaiming the Role of Story in Worship*

# Whispers from the Lord

## A Missionary Nurse's Journal

**JEFF BARKER**

an imprint of Hendrickson Publishing Group

**Whispers from the Lord: A Missionary Nurse's Journal**

Published by Hendrickson Publishers
an imprint of Hendrickson Publishing Group
Hendrickson Publishers, LLC
P. O. Box 3473
Peabody, Massachusetts 01961-3473
www.hendricksonpublishinggroup.com

978-1-4964-7619-7

Arlene Schuiteman's transcriptions of her messages received through the Holy Spirit have been edited for formatting, but in every significant way remain as she recorded them. The originals may be found within her journals and will eventually be available to researchers at the Joint Archives of Holland in Holland, Michigan. https://hope.edu/library/joint-archives-holland/

*Printed in the United States of America*

*First Printing — March 2023*

Library of Congress Control Number: 2022944614

*For Karissa,*
*faithful detective*
*and superb storyteller*

*Your cross may oppress you today,*
*but it will transfigure you tomorrow and*
*lift you up to heaven. Value it highly.*

Basilea Schlink

# Contents

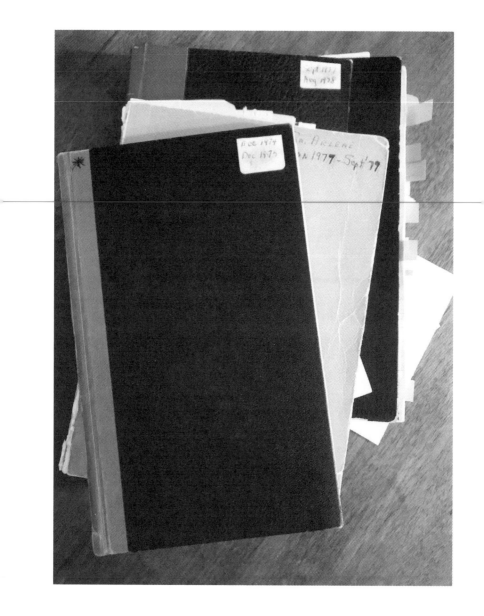

# ✚ Introduction: The Quest

What does it mean to seek God with your whole heart? What follows is a glimpse into one woman's journey. Here is an affirmation of God's deep knowledge of his children and his loving care for them.

## Background

Arlene Schuiteman was born in 1924 in a little white farmhouse north of Sioux Center, Iowa. She was the tallest of John and Johanna Schuiteman's six daughters and the only one who never married. She was desired by more than one man, and she would have been pleased to become a farmer's wife and raise a family. Instead, she remained true to God's call on her life, which for her never included becoming a wife. She was called to remain single and, through her Christian denomination (the Reformed Church in America), assigned to medical missions on the African continent.

Arlene's home church wholeheartedly supported her call to missions. Although her pastors and elders acknowledged the power of the Holy Spirit, their reverence of the Spirit didn't evidence itself in any charismatic displays. Ironically, it was during a worship service at that very church when Arlene experienced a supernatural, physical "glowing" from head to toe. From that moment forward, her prayer life changed and she became open to continuing manifestations of the Holy Spirit. That openness would later come to Pentecostal fruition during the Ethiopian revival of the 1970s.

Arlene's stoic, Dutch upbringing continued to serve as a moderating influence even as she had numerous experiences of the supernatural world. Never quick to react, though, she tested everything with careful thought and much prayer. Disciplines—such as the study of the Scriptures, corporate worship, fellowship, fasting, music, the arts, and journaling—served to bring her clarity and calm as she lived within the realm of miracles, exorcisms, and prophecies. She leaned on the mentorship of family members, pastors, Christian friends, and the best books she could get her hands on. Through these disciplines, Arlene confirmed her call and Christian walk.

Obedience to her missional call became her lifelong priority, and she studied to be a nurse with the specific motivation to practice on a foreign field as a medical missionary. Her career as a missionary nurse began in rural South Sudan in 1955. It was there, at the clinic along the Sobat River in Nasir, that Arlene was given the Nuer name of "Nya BiGoaa Jon," meaning "Miss You-will-be-good, Daughter of John." The name stuck. Nya BiGoaa is what her missionary colleagues continued to call her, and Nya BiGoaa appears in Nuer oral and written histories.

During the civil unrest of the 1960s, the north Sudanese government forced Arlene out of the country, and she returned to Iowa to finish a degree in public health. In 1966, she accepted an invitation to open a nursing school in western Ethiopia. Her school and hospital were in the town of Mettu, Ethiopia, close to the border between Ethiopia and South Sudan, so she often encountered old friends from Nasir.

While Arlene was teaching in Ethiopia's western mountains, there was a great spiritual revival. Arlene herself was filled with the Holy Spirit and received the gift of tongues, which became a personal prayer discipline she has continued to practice throughout her life. In Mettu, Arlene attended a Presbyterian church, but it was unlike any Presbyterian congregation she ever imagined! Worship was long, passionate, and loud, filled with shouting and dancing. Prayers were offered and often answered with immediate miracles similar to the healings, exorcisms, and prophecies recorded in the Gospels and the book of Acts.

Although Arlene didn't consider herself a prophetess, her mountain village church practiced public prophetic utterance. Arlene believed that God spoke to and through his servants in the contemporary age, but she never spoke a public prophecy. She affirmed, though, that the Spirit of God had given her gifts, including the gift of discernment. She could discern when the threat of a demon was real. With a nurse's heart, she rushed to pray for and physically support any person who wailed and thrashed at the start of an exorcism. In addition, she believed she could discern whether someone's prophecy was authentic or motivated by attention seeking. Though she chose not to speak aloud to denounce false prophets, she readily prayed against them.

During the religious revival of the 1970s, Ethiopia suffered from starvation and violent revolution. When the younger generation blamed the country's centuries-old feudal system of governance, the emperor was overthrown and the military leaders turned away from the United States and toward the Soviet Union. The winds of change were blowing, and Arlene was eventually asked to leave the country.

## Journals, Scriptures, and Messages

Throughout her adult life, Arlene kept a personal journal. Her journals penned on the mission field helped her remember details for writing letters home. But her journaling also helped her keep track of spiritual disciplines—the Scriptures she studied, the sermons she heard, the books she read, fasting, worship, and her personal prayer activities. Then, in midsummer 1975, her journal took on a new aspect as she began to record messages that God was speaking directly to her.

Arlene doesn't remember how she began the process of writing these special messages in her journal. She was certainly aware of the role of prophecy in Scripture, and she had also witnessed many spoken prophecies at her church in Mettu, but she knew nothing about the practice of prophetic writing—until July 1, 1975, when she felt the Spirit of God communicate directly to her. For Arlene, these personal messages typically had the following characteristics:

1. They were extensions of the Scriptures Arlene was studying.

2. They applied to Arlene's specific situation.

3. They had a universal, almost poetic quality, which makes their wisdom useful to other Christ-followers.

The messages that began on that July day continued sporadically over the next four years. She didn't follow this writing practice glibly or forcibly. The messages sometimes came in waves, appearing nearly every day in her journal. Then days or even weeks would go by with no message.

Arlene recorded in her journals ninety messages that God spoke directly to her—words of comfort, counsel, and conviction. These messages reveal her intimate and trusting relationship with the Lover of her soul. Those ninety occasions are recorded here along with their original context. Interestingly, eleven of the occasions are repeated earlier messages (65–70, 75, 79, 84, 86, and 88). Unfortunately, Arlene didn't explain in her journals her process for choosing which messages to repeat—and at this late stage in her life, she can no longer recall the reason why certain messages were repeated.

## Suggestions for Using This Book

The point of sharing these "whispers" as recorded in Arlene's journals is to encourage your own walk with God. Arlene's intimacy with her Savior is her own, but these divine messages may be intended for you as well. Such a possibility should be considered and tested.

As Arlene recorded the messages, she believed that any prophecy should be tested against Scripture and within the crucible of prayer and a life of Christian discipline. Biblical prophecies arose in specific historical contexts, and those contexts should always be examined as part of the quest for understanding Scripture. The same examination of context holds true for these messages that Arlene received.

Arlene received the first messages in a mountain village in western Ethiopia. The messages followed her move to the capital city of Addis Ababa, came home with her to the United States (Iowa and Kentucky), and finally returned briefly to her on the African continent.

The larger story of Arlene's time in Africa may be found in a trilogy of books, beginning with *Sioux Center Sudan*, which tells of Arlene's time in Nasir, South Sudan. Her story continues in the village of Mettu with the book *Iowa Ethiopia* and concludes her career in Macha with *Zambia Home*. In this present book, a small amount of specific context is provided along with each of the ninety messages. As you contemplate the circumstances in which God spoke to Arlene, ask God whether the message to her contains truth for you as well.

The ninety handwritten messages included here are as she wrote them with only occasional and minor editing. Various idiosyncrasies, such as underlining and capital letters, are left intact. If you want to see the originals, you will eventually be able to access Arlene's journals and letters at the Joint Archives of Holland in Holland, Michigan (https://hope.edu/library/joint-archives-holland/).

The Scripture passages that precede each journal entry are most often passages Arlene recorded in her journal on that date (although for Message 7, it was the day before). Sometimes the passages that Arlene cited have been expanded by a few verses to provide context. On the few occasions that Arlene didn't record a passage, the chosen Scriptures are from that date in *Daily Light on the Daily Path*, a devotional guide Arlene used (Messages 12, 30, 35, and 44). Some Scriptures were chosen based on biblical allusions within the message itself (19, 24, 26, 36, 38, 41, 74, and 90).

The Bible translations used in this book are the same that Arlene used. At the time she transcribed these messages, she didn't have many of the Bible translations she would later be able to access. During these years, she read Scripture in Dutch, the King James Version, the Revised Standard Version, The Living Bible, the New Heart English Bible, as well as translations of the various languages of the countries in which she served as a medical missionary. Occasionally, for purposes of current biblical scholarship, this book switches from the RSV or the TLB versions Arlene used to the New Revised Standard Version or the New Living Translation. To maintain the original aspect of her journal writing and the flow of the text, there are no verse numbers included with the Scripture passages.

Read slowly. There is much to contemplate here. It might be best to read one entry per day, taking three months to get through the book. Then start over, using Arlene's correspondence with her Comforter to further encourage your own love of your Savior.

As you notice the context in which Arlene wrote these ninety messages, consider how the message she received may relate to your own life circumstances. Keep your Bible and journal beside you. Ask the Spirit to prompt your reflections. Questions are provided to encourage your thinking and also to help with small group discussion. You might sometimes write as Arlene did, asking the Spirit to speak directly to you. You might also consider writing prayers of response: express your love to the Lord, confess sins, list what you are thankful for, and state your requests. Use the disciplines of listening, repetition, and contemplation to most effectively receive the great treasures once given to Arlene and now offered to a new generation.

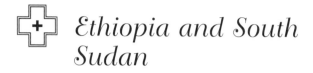

# Ethiopia and South Sudan

# 1975

## July 1 to November 13

Roger Den Herder died June 10th and Gladys
Vermeer June 4th both of CANCER - both
younger than I.

"Jeremiah 17:7-10 Blessed is the man
who trusts in the Lord, whose trust is
the Lord".

"My child, you have been deceived in your
heart by the enemy who is always seeking
to discourage and confuse, You are not
thinking My thoughts after Me. You are confusing
the issues. My wisdom is often foolishness
to those who do not Know Me. But you do
know Me, and Satan can have no part in you
when you walk in My Light. Do not listen to
false insinuations of fear and weariness.
He cannot deceive My children if they claim
My tower over each decision or situation.
Do not wait for his attack - claim My
Wisdom in advance!" Amen -- Hallelujah -
Praise you Jesus. THANK YOU

# ✚ *Message 1*

Blessed are those who trust in the LORD,
    whose trust is the LORD.
They shall be like a tree planted by water,
    sending out its roots by the stream.
It shall not fear when heat comes,
    and its leaves shall stay green;
in the year of drought it is not anxious,
    and it does not cease to bear fruit.

The heart is devious above all else;
    ~~it is perverse—~~
    who can understand it?
I the LORD test the mind
    and search the heart,
to give to all according to their ways,
    according to the fruit of their doings.
                       Jeremiah 17:7–10 (NRSVue)

In the summer of 1975, Arlene was in her ninth year as director of Mettu Hospital Dresser School (nursing school) in the western mountains of Ethiopia. That summer, many regions of Ethiopia suffered from drought and horrendous famine, and there were rumors of war. Emperor Haile Selassie had been deposed in a military coup and was now imprisoned in the basement of his palace. A Socialist government (called the Derg) was slowly taking shape, bringing persecution to the charismatic Christians with whom Arlene was allied. Military planes buzzed threateningly low, creating panic in the village.

Arlene loved her church in Mettu. Worship there was fervent and authentic. However, the leaders of the church were battling over finances. Through either ineptitude or theft, significant sums had disappeared. So, in spite of electrifying worship services, the church leadership council (of which Arlene was a member) was holding angry meetings that went deep into the night.

Arlene was also on call at the hospital that June. On the final Sunday of the month, there were three difficult births, followed by a car accident with seven patients having "the usual cuts, bruises, and fractures." Arlene had a bad cold, but weary as she was, she crossed the wide lawn between her home and the hospital to join the crew to work into the night.

By the following Tuesday, when Arlene sat down with her Bible and journal, she was on a ragged edge. She was reading the book of Jeremiah in which the words of the prophet flowed easily back and forth between the prophet's speech about God and direct speech from God. Suddenly, Arlene's own journaling matched Jeremiah's pattern, flowing from her own words into God's words. This was the first occasion on which she recorded in her journal God speaking directly to her.

*July 1, 1975, Tuesday*

> *My child, you have been deceived in your heart by the enemy who is always seeking to discourage and confuse. You are not thinking My thoughts after Me. You are confusing the issues. My wisdom is often foolishness to those who do not know Me. But you do know Me, and Satan can have no part in you when you walk in My Light. Do not listen to false insinuations of fear and weariness. He cannot deceive My children if they claim My Power over each decision or situation. Do not wait for his attack—claim My Wisdom in advance!*

After recording the message, Arlene wrote just below it,

> *Amen. Hallelujah. Praise you Jesus. THANK YOU!*

## ✚ Questions for Reflection/Discussion

1. You are meeting Arlene here as a fifty-one-year-old nurse, teacher, and Christian. What do you already observe about her personality and practices?

2. What do you suppose it might have been about Message 1 that inspired such effusive gratitude from Arlene?

3. In the Jeremiah passage Arlene was reading that Tuesday, what is especially meaningful for you?

# *Message 2*

Therefore, put on every piece of God's armor so you will be able to resist the enemy in the time of evil. Then after the battle you will still be standing firm. Stand your ground, putting on the belt of truth and the body armor of God's righteousness. For shoes, put on the peace that comes from the Good News so that you will be fully prepared. In addition to all of these, hold up the shield of faith to stop the fiery arrows of the devil. Put on salvation as your helmet, and take the sword of the Spirit, which is the word of God.

Pray in the Spirit at all times and on every occasion. Stay alert and be persistent in your prayers for all believers everywhere.

Ephesians 6:13–18 (NLT)

Arlene began to sense the Holy Spirit more and more at work in her daily life. Following the Spirit's leading, she arranged for a private meeting with one of the elders of the church. Instead of outlining an agenda, she simply asked if they could begin with a time of prayer. After this, she felt that the Spirit wanted her to confront this elder about the jealousy between him and another leader. She surprised herself by speaking with real authority. She left it at that, uncertain as to what would happen next.

The following morning, during her personal devotions, she then sensed the Holy Spirit urging her to seek forgiveness from one of her students. She went that day to the student and asked forgiveness, weeping as she did so. After the student forgave her, she experienced a sense of real peace.

That weekend, there was a spiritual life conference in a nearby town. As there was a gasoline shortage, Arlene couldn't use the mission vehicle. She was grateful to get the last seat in that day's only remaining taxi. She arrived in time for the worship service that lasted four hours. The singing was so enthusiastic, she couldn't even hear the musical instruments.

The following Tuesday, one of the elders of the church stopped at her home and poured out a heartfelt confession. That night,

Arlene caught up with her journaling, briefly summarizing the past few days, and ending with this second message from the Lord:

*July 8, 1975, Tuesday*

> *You are going through a <u>tunnel</u> of grief and pain for the situations and persons around you. How much greater is My grief for them! Let your spirit reach up to Me and then out to these others. <u>In union with Me</u> your prayers for them will be more effective. Your desires for them will be channeled in My directions—not your own! Put all these burdens on Me, and I will give you rest. Let go and let Me take this responsibility that weighs so heavily on your heart. You cannot lift their loads for them. But <u>through you</u> (as you abide in Me), I can lift these persons into My greater reality and situations will change. Pray for them in the Spirit, letting My Spirit—in union with yours— pray through you.*

## ✛ Questions for Reflection/Discussion

1. Arlene attended a four-hour worship service. When have you spent several hours in worship?

2. When is a time that you asked someone for forgiveness?

3. Message 2 uses the phrase "As you abide in Me." What has it meant for you to abide in the Lord?

# ✚ *Message 3*

Those who trust in the LORD are like Mount Zion,
  which cannot be moved but abides forever.
As the mountains surround Jerusalem,
  so the LORD surrounds his people
  from this time on and forevermore.
For the scepter of wickedness shall not rest
  on the land allotted to the righteous,
so that the righteous might not stretch out
  their hands to do wrong.
Do good, O LORD to those who are good
  and to those who are upright in their hearts.
But those who turn aside to their own crooked ways,
  the LORD will lead away with evildoers.
  Peace be upon Israel!

                              Psalm 125 (NRSVue)

Starting on Saturday, the irritants began piling up. First, Arlene took a trip to the market and discovered there wasn't any food to buy. Then, on Monday morning, she arrived at school to learn that the students were on strike over a quarrel between the government and the school administrators regarding the stipend amounts due each student while they were taking classes and also working over at the hospital. There would be neither schooling nor nursing today.

Striking was becoming a common tactic throughout the country, and Arlene expected more strikes that autumn, especially if the Derg government persisted in its plan of *Zemacha* (an Amharic term referring to a military-style campaign). The *Zemacha* would necessitate the closing of secondary schools and colleges (including Arlene's school) and the forcing of students to travel from town to town and farm to farm to indoctrinate peasants in the goals of the revolution. Arlene expected her students to rebel against the planned *Zemacha*. While she was not delighted with the government's plan, she was not inclined to take a political position.

Late that afternoon on the day of the school strike, Arlene drove across the mountain to the church building. Since the road had been quite dry when she walked to worship the day before, she thought it would be safe to take the mission's Volkswagen to the Monday meeting. That turned out to be a bad decision. On her way home, Arlene encountered enough rain to make the clay mountain road as slippery as ice. She spun out and barely kept from sliding down the mountainside. Although she managed to arrive home safely, she determined not to drive again until the rainy season ended in October. On top of all of this, the meeting at the church had not gone well. The simmering disagreement among the leaders finally burst into a flame of angry words, even from the pastor.

At the end of that disconcerting day, her home was a welcome place of peace. She pulled out her Bible and journal, and the Spirit began to speak.

*July 14, 1975, Monday*

> *Fear not, My child, the works of darkness—for my arms are round about you like the mountains encircling Jerusalem. You are protected as you continue to trust in Me. Abide in Me. As you ask for My Presence to enter into you today in this deep stillness, a layer of Peace is being formed within you so that the irritations and frustrations of the day* cannot *come through to harm your spirit.*

## ✚ Questions for Reflection/Discussion

1. What were the irritations and frustrations that threatened to harm Arlene's spirit on this occasion?

2. What physical location helps you find "deep stillness"?

3. How would you recognize that "a layer of Peace" was being formed within you?

 *Message 4*

Now when they heard these things they were enraged, and they ground their teeth against him. But he, full of the Holy Spirit, gazed into heaven and saw the glory of God, and Jesus standing at the right hand of God; and he said, "Behold, I see the heavens opened, and the Son of man standing at the right hand of God." But they cried out with a loud voice and stopped their ears and rushed together upon him. Then they cast him out of the city and stoned him; and the witnesses laid down their garments at the feet of a young man named Saul. And as they were stoning Stephen, he prayed, "Lord Jesus, receive my spirit." And he knelt down and cried with a loud voice, "Lord, do not hold this sin against them." And when he had said this, he fell asleep.

Acts 7:54–60 (RSV)

On a rainy Thursday afternoon, Arlene was resting on her porch when she saw a man she knew from church walking toward her. She invited him to come up and sit, but he said he had only come to deliver a letter. He handed her a thick envelope and then hurried away. Opening the envelope, she found a handwritten letter that began, "To dear Christian Sister Miss Arlene." Nine pages later, despite the writer ending the letter saying he never intended to harm her, he had made many accusations, including that she had been carrying on an illicit relationship with a leader in the church. His stunning accusations against her in the letter proved she was anything but dear to him. If these accusations were true, she told herself, then she must leave Mettu and never return. Although she knew the accusations were false, she couldn't bring herself to simply toss aside this letter. In her journal, she wrote that his words *injured, wounded, pierced, and HURT*.

The next day, she left town to give entrance exams at Gambela, which allowed her to put the letter mostly out of her mind. When she returned home several days later, she read the letter again and it brought "deep pain" to her heart. She decided that the best course of action would be to write out a succinct summary of the accusations and ask the Lord if there was any truth in them. After she did this, she saw no truth in the writer's words. Nevertheless, she placed the list in God's care by scrawling in large print over the entire page in block letters with red ink:

*BLOOD of <u>JESUS</u>*

The last entry she wrote in her journal that night was this Scripture:

> I advise you, O daughter, not to fret about your parents in your homeland far away. Your royal husband delights in your beauty. Reverence him, for he is your lord.
> Psalm 45:10-11 (TLB)

The next morning, she still felt angry with the man for falsely accusing her. Then she received this message:

*July 30, 1975, Wednesday*

> *Do not become bitter, My child, because of those who have turned against you to persecute you. The jealousy of cruel men crucified me. Like Stephen the martyr you have been stoned by these lies, but you have not been put to death. Can you pray as he did that their sins not be held against them? Can you forgive those who persecute you? Let Me win the victory as you forgive them for their sins. Your resentments will hurt you—not them. A bitter heart poisons your whole body. <u>Forgive</u>. Want to forgive as I forgive!!*

After writing the message in her journal, Arlene went about her daily teaching duties, but she remained deeply troubled. She wasn't able to obey the message. She knew she must forgive, but she didn't yet *want* to forgive.

That night when she laid her head on her pillow, she was completely exhausted and fell immediately asleep. Then, at midnight, the sound of knocking woke her; but when she went to the door, no one was there. She later believed it was Jesus who had awakened her. At 2:00 that morning, she wrote a long prayer, including the following:

> *Father—God of Abraham, Isaac, and Jacob—*
> *You are Pure Light with no shadow of turning.*
> *You are Pure Truth.*
> *You are ALL-knowing.*
> *You are Ultimate Power.*
> *You are Perfect Judge.*
> *There is no need to hide anything from You. I am not trying*
> *to hide anything from You. I am not trying to hide from*
> *You. But I know that the human heart is the most deceitful*
> *thing there is.*
> *God, I, too am human—flesh—of the same dust as Eve. Search*
> *me, O my God, and know my heart. You know, my All-*
> *knowing and All-seeing God, that there has never been*
> *ANY act of sexual immorality between him and me, or*
> *anyone else.*
> *Jesus, free me from any and all self-justification,*
> *rationalizations, self-righteousness, hypocrisy, self-*
> *deception, bitterness.*
> *Dearest Jesus—Savior, Redeemer, Sanctifier, Lover—You are*
> *my first Love . . . no one between.*
> *Yes, God, I have been proud of my name and tried to keep*
> *my reputation respectable. Are you asking me to sacrifice*
> *my name? Amen. So be it. Jesus, baptize me with your*
> *compassion and love for others.*
> *Dear Jesus, what do I do? Jesus, I don't want to ever see*
> *him. You know the depth of the pain. Make me want to*
> *forgive him. Jesus, cleanse my unforgiving spirit with your*
> *BLOOD. Thank you, Jesus, it was for me that you suffered*
> *in Gethsemane—and on the way to the cross—and on the*
> *cross—and you never sinned. You didn't have to do it but*
> *You did it out of Love and obedience to the Father. Jesus,*
> *cover me with your clean robe of righteousness and present*
> *me before the Holy Father now. I place myself on the altar of*
> *sacrifice. All I have to give is my love. Take it and use me as*
> *you wish.*

She didn't go back to sleep. She would later write,

> *How tenderly and graciously He dealt with me the rest of that night until daybreak only He and I know.*

## Questions for Reflection/Discussion

1. What were the various evidences that Arlene was truly wounded?

2. What experience do you have of being wrongly accused?

3. Arlene felt asked to let go of her reputation. Can you think of a time when that was your experience?

 *Message 5*

As the sun rose the next morning, Arlene wrote this prayer in her journal:

*Sweet Holy Spirit, fill in all the empty places of my being with peace, with love, with forgiveness, with joy, with health, with energy, with wisdom, with faith, and with trust. Help me to walk as Jesus's disciple in the yoke with Him.*

*Your obedient one,*
*Arlene*

As part of her daily devotions, Arlene would read the collected Scriptures from the nineteenth-century guidebook *Daily Light on the Daily Path*. That Thursday morning's entry included seven biblical passages about suffering. Arlene looked up two of the references in her copy of The Living Bible and copied verses from that paraphrase into her journal:

Take your share of suffering as a good soldier of Jesus Christ.

2 Timothy 2:3a

After you have suffered a little while, our God, who is full of kindness through Christ, will give you his eternal glory. He personally will come and pick you up, and set you firmly in place, and make you stronger than ever.

1 Peter 5:10

Then her focus turned outward as she recalled the parable of the gathering of the nations:

"Then the King will say to those on his right, 'Come, you who are blessed by my Father, inherit the Kingdom prepared for you from the creation of the world. For I was hungry, and you fed me. I was thirsty, and you gave me a drink. I was a stranger, and you invited me into your home. I was naked, and you gave me clothing. I was sick, and you cared for me. I was in prison, and you visited me.'

"Then these righteous ones will reply, 'Lord, when did we ever see you hungry and feed you? Or thirsty and give you something to drink? Or a stranger and show you hospitality? Or naked and give you clothing? When did we ever see you sick or in prison and visit you?'

"And the King will say, 'I tell you the truth, when you did it to one of the least of these my brothers and sisters, you were doing it to me!'"

Matthew 25:34–40 (NLT)

Then came this message from her Comforter:

*July 31, 1975, Thursday*

*Give this one who has hurt you a cup of cold water in My Name. Remember that whatever you do to him you are doing unto Me. In turning the other cheek, you will win him to Me. My Love will enable you to be Love in this difficult situation. It is not as hopeless as you think. My Love avails much. Forgive him—even as I have forgiven you.*

Before going to bed that night, Arlene wrote this prayer and response in her journal:

*Jesus, your faithfulness and your LOVE and your Presence during the hours of this long day fill my heart with joy, praise, and thanksgiving. "Oh for a thousand tongues to sing."*

*I'm not weary or exhausted after being up since 2 AM. Jesus gave me such peace, joy, and assurance of His constant Presence walking beside me carrying my burdens today. His yoke IS EASY!*

## ✚ Questions for Reflection/Discussion

1. What were the specific practices Arlene used to assist herself spiritually and emotionally over the previous two days?

2. What practices do you use to strengthen your spiritual life?

3. What does it mean to be "in the yoke" with Jesus?

 *Message 6*

"Come, let us return to the Lord; it is he who has torn us—he will heal us. He has wounded—he will bind us up. In just a couple of days, or three at the most, he will set us on our feet again to live in his kindness! Oh, that we might know the Lord! Let us press on to know him, and he will respond to us as surely as the coming of dawn or the rain of early spring.

"O Ephraim and Judah, what shall I do with you? For your love vanishes like morning clouds, and disappears like dew. I sent my prophets to warn you of your doom; I have slain you with the words of my mouth, threatening you with death. Suddenly, without warning, my judgment will strike you as surely as day follows night.

"I don't want your sacrifices—I want your love; I don't want your offerings—I want you to know me."

Hosea 6:1–6 (TLB)

Arlene was nearing the end of a long and wearying week. She hadn't yet told any of her friends, colleagues, or family about the accusing letter. Instead, she continued to pour out her heart to the Lord and go about her business of teaching, nursing, and administrating the school. She held a three-hour meeting to begin choosing the sixteen students of the incoming class of future dressers from among the many applicants.

That evening, a leader from the church stopped by for a friendly visit. Arlene took this opportunity to tell him she wanted to meet with the elders, deacons, and deaconesses. She only told him that it was a matter for which she needed counsel. The elder said he would speak with Pastor Terfa as soon as he returned from a short trip.

On Friday morning around 6:00, Arlene poured some of her prayer onto the pages of her journal:

*Yes, Lord, Lover. You do respond to us as sure as the coming of dawn. Hold on to me—all my being and my sense and my desires—so that my love will not vanish like the morning clouds or disappear as the dew.*

*Master—please—today—walk beside me and help me face and carry the burdens of the day. "Let justice roll down like waters and righteousness like an ever-flowing stream." Amos 5:24*

The Spirit of God responded:

*August 1, 1975, Friday*

*My justice is sufficient for you. My righteousness will be like an ever-flowing stream. A forgiving heart is a greater sacrifice to Me than burnt offerings. My justice cannot be evaded: it will roll down like waters. Let Me bring good out of this situation as you forgive the one who has hurt you. Judgment is Mine—not yours.*

With that, Arlene was off to a busy morning at school. She spent her lunch hour at the hospital, assisting in the delivery of a beautiful, healthy boy. That evening, she wrote letters and an article for the mission's newsletter *Ethio Echo*. She then ended the day by penning this prayer in her journal:

*Father, my mind boggles as I try to think of You.*

1. *You never sleep.*

2. *You never forget Your promises.*

3. *Your compassion never ends.*

4. *You will never let me stumble, slip, or fall.*

5. *You know the number of hairs on my head.*

6. *You are full of tenderness and mercy.*

7. *You shine on me with beams of love.*

8. *Your lovingkindness is flowing like a river.*

9. *Your benevolence surrounds and supports me.*

*My inward emotions are moved with gratitude as my spirit remembers, meditates and thinks upon Your goodness, O my Father.*

## ✚ Questions for Reflection/Discussion

1. In the first verses of Hosea 6, who is saying of God, "In just a couple of days, or three at the most, he will set us on our feet again to live in his kindness"? What does God think of their glibness?

2. In what ways did Arlene leave justice to the Lord, and what actions did she take to address the circumstances?

3. Message 6 says, "A forgiving heart is a greater sacrifice to Me than burnt offerings." In what way could forgiveness be understood as an act of worship?

 *Message 7*

Praise the Lord if you are punished for doing right! Of course, you get no credit for being patient if you are beaten for doing wrong; but if you do right and suffer for it, and are patient beneath the blows, God is well pleased.

This suffering is all part of the work God has given you. Christ, who suffered for you, is your example. Follow in his steps: He never sinned, never told a lie, never answered back when insulted; when he suffered he did not threaten to get even; he left his case in the hands of God who always judges fairly. He personally carried the load of our sins in his own body when he died on the cross so that we can be finished with sin and live a good life from now on. For his wounds have healed ours!

1 Peter 2:19b–24 (TLB)

The word *jealousy* held special meaning for Arlene. The previous December, a prophecy had been spoken at church that specifically stated that four persons needed to repent of their jealousy. Arlene felt that she was one of the four. She had detected the first danger signs of jealousy when she noticed that sometimes one of her male friends at church visited others and did not stop by to see her. She knew the dangers of jealousy for herself and the church:

> For where jealousy and selfish ambition exist, there will be disorder and every vile practice. But the wisdom from above is first pure, then peaceable, gentle, open to reason, full of mercy and good fruits, without uncertainty or insincerity. And the harvest of righteousness is sown in peace by those who make peace.

James 3:16–18 (RSV)

With tears, Arlene had confessed her jealousy to the Lord. Now, all these months later, her close friendship with that man was being thrown back in her face through the accuser's letter. She did not know how she could defend herself since only she and God knew her heart. Then she received this confirmation that God was enough.

*August 3, 1975, Sunday*

> *Remember that no one else can fulfill the place that has been prepared for you if you walk in My Love. <u>You</u> <u>must</u> <u>be</u> <u>patient</u> so that My Plans for you can unfold. In kindness to all, in humility (not boastfulness), you will find a new Peace in your life. When you live in a spirit of My Love, there is no room for jealousy.*

## ✚ Questions for Reflection/Discussion

1. Arlene's Mettu church allowed time for prophetic utterance during worship. Have you had any experience of prophecy spoken in a public gathering? If so, what did you think about it?

2. What biblical prophecies have been especially meaningful to you?

3. Message 7 says, "You must be patient so that My Plans for you can unfold." When have you experienced the value of waiting for the Lord?

# Message 8

> For I know the plans I have for you, says the LORD, plans for welfare and not for evil, to give you a future and a hope. Then you will call upon me and come and pray to me, and I will hear you.
>
> Jeremiah 29:11–12 (RSV)

After a restful Sunday, Arlene felt calmer. She expected that sometime soon Pastor Terfa would be available for a meeting with the elders concerning the accusations that had been made against her. On the pages of her journal, she asked, *What will the elders advise—to expose the letter or to drop it?* As much as she was praying for grace and a forgiving spirit, she found herself on the lookout for her accuser and any of his close friends, wondering how they would respond to her if their paths crossed.

Tuesday was a difficult day. At 5:00 a.m., Arlene was called to assist in the delivery of a baby born with anencephaly, a condition in which parts of the brain and skull are not formed. The child lived for only three hours. That afternoon, two church leaders stopped by to say that an elders meeting had been called to consider a letter they had received from her accuser. Although they weren't asking Arlene to be present at the meeting, they asked if they could see the letter she had received.

She retrieved it and read it to them, weeping as she did so. They attempted to encourage her, but they all knew that the congregation's love for one another was about to be tested. The men left for the meeting, and Arlene was called back to the emergency room for a *placenta previa* case. It was too late—the obstruction was too great. Both mother and child died that night.

When Arlene finally crawled into bed, she had not yet learned the results of the elders meeting. When she arose for Wednesday prayers, she received this message from the Lord:

*August 6, 1975, Wednesday*

*Your faith is growing daily through these testings which I am giving you grace to overcome. I did not promise you a life of ease but a cross to bear with Me. I, too, was persecuted—far more than you—by the jealousy, and anger, and spitefulness of others. Be steadfast in your faith and in your love one for another. My church will be persecuted by the world, but I have overcome the world.*

## ✚ Questions for Reflection/Discussion

1. What were the various pressures on Arlene's emotions at this time?

2. When did Jesus experience the jealousy of others?

3. Message 8 says, "My church will be persecuted." What experience have you had with persecution?

# Message 9

We should help others do what is right and build them up in the Lord. For even Christ didn't live to please himself. As the Scriptures say, "The insults of those who insult you, O God, have fallen on me." Such things were written in the Scriptures long ago to teach us. And the Scriptures give us hope and encouragement as we wait patiently for God's promises to be fulfilled. May God, who gives this patience and encouragement, help you live in complete harmony with each other, as is fitting for followers of Christ Jesus. Then all of you can join together with one voice, giving praise and glory to God, the Father of our Lord Jesus Christ.

I pray that God, the source of hope, will fill you completely with joy and peace because you trust in him. Then you will overflow with confident hope through the power of the Holy Spirit.

Romans 15:2–6, 13 (NLT)

On Wednesday evening, one of the elders stopped by Arlene's house to report that the letter they received from her accuser was similar to the one she had shared with him the previous day. He wasn't there to speak on behalf of the church but simply to encourage her as best he could. They prayed and then he left.

Despite being desperately tired, she didn't sleep well that night. At 1:30 in the morning, she was awake, writing.

*August 7, 1975, Thursday*

*You wonder at the spirit of rebellion and lawlessness that is possessing humanity. You cringe at the false prophets and heresies that have entered even into My churches at times. I warned you that this would be so in the last days when the prince of this world would make his last attempt to seduce and destroy. But when I return in power, I will destroy the works of the enemy, and you shall be lifted up with Me in glory—you who remain faithful to Me, who love the Truth, and who put all your trust in Me shall be saved.*

Arlene responded to the message by writing ten declarations of what faithfulness, love, and trust meant to her:

1. *Let no person cause my love for Jesus to be divided. From now onwards.*

2. *Let no <u>things</u> cause my love for Jesus to be divided. From now onwards.*

3. *Let there be no pride.*

4. *Let there be no hypocrisy.*

5. *Let there be no lust or impure thoughts.*

6. *Let there be no gossip or critical tongue.*

7. *Let there be no fear.*

8. *Let there be no jealousy.*

9. *Let there be no self-pity.*

10. *Let there be no unforgiving spirit in me.*

At some point that night, she finally fell asleep. Later in the day, she prepared a syllabus for the upcoming school term. She met with the household workers threatening to go on strike. She visited with friends. But she didn't hear anything more from the church regarding the elders meeting. She was uncertain she ever would.

## ✠ *Questions for Reflection/Discussion*

1. Arlene wrote ten declarations: "Let there be no . . ." Is there anyone in your life (or even yourself) who has written such personal declarations?

2. Look again at Arlene's declarations. How might you re-write them into positive phrasings: "Let there be . . ."

3. Have you ever woken in the night to pray and perhaps write down your prayer or thoughts?

## Message 10

Grace to you and peace from God our Father, and the Lord Jesus Christ, who gave himself for our sins, that he might deliver us out of this present evil age, according to the will of our God and Father—to whom be the glory forever and ever. Amen.

I am astonished that you are so quickly deserting him who called you by the grace of Christ to a different "good news"; and there is not another "good news." Only there are some who trouble you, and want to pervert the Good News of Christ. But even though we, or an angel from heaven, should proclaim to you a "good news" other than that which we preached to you, let him be cursed. As we have said before, so I now say again: if anyone preaches to you a "good news" other than that which you received, let him be cursed.

For am I now seeking the favor of people, or of God? Or am I striving to please people? For if I were still pleasing people, I would not be a servant of Christ.

Galatians 1:3–10 (NHEB)

At noon the next day, Pastor Terfa visited Arlene. She knew he had been at the elders meeting earlier that week, and so she poured out her heart to him. Like the pastor he was, he ministered to her in a real way. When he left, she wrote this prayer in her journal:

> *Jesus—I don't want my love for you to be <u>divided</u>. If I am still chained to earthly possessions, to my honor, to my profession, to any person, please, Jesus, break the chains. I want to be at the Marriage Feast of the Lamb as your bridal lover.*

Then God spoke to her.

*August 8, 1975, Friday*

> *You have refused to take on the unrighteousness of the world and its false gods and perverted signs and wonders. You are being sanctified by My indwelling Spirit, the Holy Comforter,*

*whom I have sent to lead you into all Truth, to strengthen your witness. Continue to hold steadfastly to My Promises so that you may be with me in glory when that awe-full day of My return comes.*

The following day was cold and rainy. Arlene stayed home, wrote letters, read, and rested. She did not record any Scriptures in her journal that day, and there were no more messages that week. The saga of the accusations seemed to be nearing an end.

## Questions for Reflection/Discussion

1. Who has been a minister to you the way that Pastor Terfa was to Arlene?

2. Arlene prayed, "If I am still chained to . . . please, Jesus, break the chains." Do you resonate with that request? Have you ever experienced Jesus breaking chains in your life?

3. Message 10 says, "You are being sanctified." What does "being sanctified" mean to you?

 *Message 11*

> But the Lord is faithful; he will make you strong and guard you from satanic attacks of every kind. And we trust the Lord that you are putting into practice the things we taught you, and that you always will. May the Lord bring you into an ever deeper understanding of the love of God and of the patience that comes from Christ.
>
> 2 Thessalonians 3:3–5 (TLB)

The dark Sunday morning was as cold and wet as expected for the rainy season. Since it was still too dangerous to drive on the slippery clay, Arlene walked through the rain to worship—for that's where she longed to be.

She later reported in her journal that the overflowing worship service was *ALIVE from beginning to end.* Pastor Terfa preached, and Arlene's friend Mersha led the singing and prayers. During the service, various members of the congregation stood up to offer testimonies of God at work in their lives. After each testimony, the congregation gave out a "joy-cry"—a long, almost deafening shout with an undercurrent of stomping, banging, and ululations. As if it were New Testament times, a blind man announced that he was no longer blind. He had been prayed over, and now he could see. Joy-cry! A man named Yadette had been released from prison. In those days of the Socialist government's suppression of religion, imprisonment was almost a badge of honor. Yadette explained that the prison guards had locked him in a latrine, and his simple prayer was that the smell wouldn't enter his nostrils. His prayer was answered, and he didn't smell a thing until the day he was released. Joy-cry! After the shouts died down, the congregation raised its voice in prayer. Then one woman cried out with a different kind of cry—and as was the case so many Sundays at Arlene's church, the woman was delivered of a demon then and there.

Arlene later remembered that she didn't even notice whether her accuser was present in the service. She was grateful that, at last, her focus was elsewhere. That night, Mersha stopped at her house to tell Arlene that he had spoken to her accuser—and that the accuser planned to write Arlene an apology.

*August 10, 1975, Sunday*

> *No matter how much the devil unleashes his evil powers in the world about you, there is nothing for you to fear if you remain steadfast in My Love. I have promised to be with you ALWAYS—to the very close of the age. I will direct your comings and your goings. I will protect you from the evil one. I will keep you strong in My Love, as you put your trust in Me and obey My WILL for your life. I will be with you in Power and inward Peace.*

## ✚ Questions for Reflection/Discussion

1. What were the components of the worship service that Arlene described as "alive from beginning to end"?

2. What did Paul mean when he wrote to the Thessalonian church that he hoped they were practicing what they had been taught?

3. Paul's epistle alludes to Satan and Message 11 mentions the devil as well as "the evil one." When have you observed the reality of the powers of darkness?

 *Message 12*

Do not quench the Spirit. Do not despise prophecies, but test everything; hold fast to what is good; abstain from every form of evil.

May the God of peace himself sanctify you entirely, and may your spirit and soul and body be kept sound and blameless at the coming of our Lord Jesus Christ. The one who calls you is faithful, and he will do this.

1 Thessalonians 5:19–24 (NRSVue)

Since she had a full day ahead, Arlene was up early. A dear missionary friend would be arriving at some point during the day, depending on the fickleness of the weather, Ethiopian Airline schedules, and the slippery mountain roads. A man from the Russian Embassy out of Addis Ababa was also due to arrive and spend the day touring the Mettu hospital and making arrangements for a small group of Russian medical personnel to be on loan from the USSR.

While awaiting these guests, Arlene had one more important person to host: Mister Alem from the National Ministry of Public Health, who would superintend Arlene's students in the writing of their final exams. These were the high-stakes exams for which Arlene had been preparing her students. At the end of a long day of writing, the students would turn their pages over to Mister Alem, who would marshal them to the capital city for grading. The results of the entire nation's medical school exams would be announced in about a month. Some students would be certified as medical professionals, while others would be required to repeat their schooling or simply move on to another career.

Arlene planned to end the day at a church business meeting that had been put on hold due to the previous week's discussions of accusation letters. With such a full day ahead, Arlene made certain to begin in prayer. She described that morning's time with her Lord as "wonderful."

*August 11, 1975, Monday*

> *Do not believe all that you read or hear. Test the spirits of those who prophesy. If their words are truly of Me, you will know the witness (confirmation) of My Spirit in your heart. Do not quench My Spirit. Let My gifts flow freely through you in Love to meet the needs of My body, the church. Remove from your life any hindrances, any dependencies that are not of Me. Hold firmly to whatever is good and pure in your thinking as well as your speaking and doing.*

## ✚ Questions for Reflection/Discussion

1. Mister Alem was arriving to test Arlene's students (and therefore Arlene). What is an ordeal that is coming soon in your life, and how are you preparing for it?

2. In 1 Thessalonians, Paul says to "test everything," and Message 12 says, "Do not believe all that you read or hear." What have you been reading or listening to that you would do well to test more?

3. What routines begin your typical day? Which ones are wonderful as they are, and which ones do you want to change?

 *Message 13*

With everlasting love I will have pity on you, says the Lord, your Re-deemer. Just as in the time of Noah I swore that I would never again permit the waters of a flood to cover the earth and destroy its life, so now I swear that I will never again pour out my anger on you. For the mountains may depart and the hills disappear, but my kindness shall not leave you. My promise of peace for you will never be broken, says the Lord who has mercy upon you.

Isaiah 54:8b-10 (TLB)

After the previous day's exams, Arlene gave the students the day off, although doing so required her to help out at the hospital as it was short-staffed. At 2:00 pm, she delivered a healthy baby and then spent the latter part of the day with her visiting friend, Marian. Marian was a school teacher—a talkative, good-natured fellow Iowan. She was one of the first missionaries Arlene had met when she was called to Nasir in the South Sudan some twenty years earlier.

Many friends stopped in to say hello to Marian, and Arlene made dinner for those who could stay—a habit of hospitality as old as Abraham and Sarah. It was a good, good day.

*August 12, 1975, Tuesday*

*I have called you and I will sanctify you, but you have a part to play in this lifetime's work. You must be honest with yourself and with others. You must <u>WILL</u> to be sanctified. Do not wait for Me to do the work: begin to <u>be</u> what I have called you to be—loving, forgiving, patient, full of faith. Feed on My Word— <u>not</u> your <u>resentments</u>, or doubts or fears. Then <u>do</u> <u>what</u> <u>I</u> <u>would</u> <u>do</u> in this situation; and My peace will enter your mind and spirit and body.*

## ✠ Questions for Reflection/Discussion

1. Isaiah's prophecy speaks of God's kindness that "shall not leave you." How have you experienced kindness today (whether from the Lord or from a person)?

2. When is the last time you provided a meal for someone who just stopped by?

3. Message 13 says, "I have called you." In what way has the Lord called you?

 *Message 14*

Dearest friends, when I was there with you, you were always so careful to follow my instructions. And now that I am away you must be even more careful to do the good things that result from being saved, obeying God with deep reverence, shrinking back from all that might displease him. For God is at work within you, helping you want to obey him, and then helping you do what he wants.

In everything you do, stay away from complaining and arguing so that no one can speak a word of blame against you. You are to live clean, innocent lives as children of God in a dark world full of people who are crooked and stubborn. Shine out among them like beacon lights, holding out to them the Word of Life. Then when Christ returns, how glad I will be that my work among you was so worthwhile.

Philippians 2:12–16 (TLB)

Arlene was tired. That wasn't what raised an alarm, since her schedule and responsibilities kept her on the edge of exhaustion much of the time. Her Ma and Pa's work ethic had taught her to feel a tinge of guilt if she wasn't tired at the end of most days. This week, however, she had an additional excuse for tiredness—she'd been staying up late talking with Marian.

What raised the alarm was how her legs ached night after night. She recognized the symptoms of malaria since she had contracted it dozens of times during her years in the South Sudan. But she didn't expect malaria here in the mountains. Maybe it was toxoplasmosis, caused by a food or waterborne parasite. She prescribed herself some Daraprim, which would cover her for both malaria and other possibilities. Daraprim came with the side-effect of a headache, but Arlene had learned to accept such physical side effects and mostly disregard them, just as she ignored her exhaustion. She seldom coddled anyone, least of all herself.

Arlene had crafted the art of self-discipline in almost every area of life. However, she was mature enough to know that self-discipline with a tendency toward perfectionism came with a *spiritual* side effect: pride. She knew she couldn't save herself from the human tendency toward self-congratulation. She needed help every day.

*August 15, 1975, Friday*

> *Have no fear of those in authority over you, but hold them in respect as My instruments. If you are admonished, pray to know My Spirit confirming where there is truth. But be subject in humility to My Spirit that through the Word of wisdom you may know the truth about yourself. In honesty seek discernment that you may grow through this correction to be more usable by Me.*
>
> ~~*You are predestined for salvation: accept this*~~ *totally not just at certain moments of exaltation. Put on the helmet (or hope) of salvation as you awaken each morning. Wear the shield of faith each day.*

## ✠ Questions for Reflection/Discussion

1. In Philippians, Paul promises that "God is at work within you, helping you." How is God helping you today?

2. Message 14 says to pray for the Spirit's truth "if you are admonished." What does it mean to be admonished, and when have you experienced this?

3. Arlene's danger point was pride. What's yours?

 *Message 15*

You are all children of the light and of the day, and do not belong to darkness and night. So be on your guard, not asleep like the others. Watch for his return and stay sober. Night is the time for sleep and the time when people get drunk. But let us who live in the light keep sober, protected by the armor of faith and love, and wearing as our helmet the happy hope of salvation.

For God has not chosen to pour out his anger upon us but to save us through our Lord Jesus Christ; he died for us so that we can live with him forever, whether we are dead or alive at the time of his return. So encourage each other to build each other up, just as you are already doing.

1 Thessalonians 5:5–11 (TLB)

On Thursday, two men stopped by who Arlene was delighted to see. One of them, a school principal in the capital city, hadn't visited the western mountains in a long while, and Arlene was eager to speak with him of their mutual experiences as school administrators. But Marian dominated the conversation, and the evening was soon gone. The other man was the one Arlene had held at arm's length for some time out of fear that she would again be possessive regarding him. Thus the conversation with all three of her old friends that night had a sense of disconnect, and when the evening broke up, the feeling in the air, at least for Arlene, was a sense of sadness.

On Friday morning, Arlene put Marian in a taxi to catch the plane at Gore. When she awoke on Saturday, the house was quiet and empty. While reflecting on the busyness of the past week, Arlene received this message.

*August 16, 1975, Saturday*

*Your mission in life is to encourage others in the faith. You are to build them up in My Love. Your words are to be used to edify them, not to tear down My images of what they can become. Hold carefully in faith these bundles I have given you—they*

*are precious to me. I have entrusted them to you, not to be*
*possessed by you, but to be loved by Me through you. Beware of*
*possessive love toward those I have given you to love for Me.*

Arlene knew that each person who visited her house was precious to the Lord, even more precious than they were to her. She
knew that even the writer of the accusation letter was precious to
the Lord. Arlene wished she could find the path to reconciliation
with him. She didn't want to be wary of seeing him at church or on
the streets of the town. But now, she had heard he was gone out of
the country. She didn't know if or when he would return, so how
could there ever be reconciliation?

She had an idea. She went to see her accuser's best friend. Arlene hadn't spoken to him after she received the letter, but she assumed he knew about it. She had been wondering if he had similar
feelings against Arlene, and her wonderings had made her turn
aside or glance away whenever she saw him in town or at church.

When he welcomed her into his office, she got quickly to the
point and asked him if he knew about the letter. He said he did—
that he had read it, but that he had nothing to do with writing it.
She admitted to him that she had included him in the hurt feelings
caused by the letter and that she had been avoiding him. She said
that she could no longer stand turning away and that she was sorry.
Afterwards, Arlene wrote that her joy had returned.

## ✚ *Questions for Reflection/Discussion*

1. Although Arlene wasn't able to reconcile with her accuser,
   his friend turned out to be a lifeline. What specific steps
   did Arlene take to bring about her return of joy?

2. When have you avoided someone?

3. Message 15 told Arlene that her mission in life was "to
   encourage others in the faith." Is that the mission of every
   Christian, or do you have a different mission?

# *Message 16*

"You have heard that it was said, 'You shall love your neighbor and hate your enemy.' But I say to you, Love your enemies and pray for those who persecute you, so that you may be children of your Father in heaven, for he makes his sun rise on the evil and on the good and sends rain on the righteous and on the unrighteous. For if you love those who love you, what reward do you have?"

Matthew 5:43–46a (NRSVue)

One of Arlene's influences was the Evangelical Sisterhood of Mary, a Lutheran mission organization founded in Germany as a response to World War II. Part of the sisterhood's goal was to make amends for the injustices perpetrated by the German government during the war. Arlene had met some of the sisters on their travels to Ethiopia, and she sometimes sojourned at their retreat center in Darmstadt.

Basilea Schlink was one of the sisterhood's founders and leaders. On this particular Sunday morning, Arlene was reading one of Mother Basilea's many books, *You Will Never Be the Same*. Its topic was the Christian's battle against sin. Today, Arlene had reached the chapter about bondage to idols. She copied large portions of the chapter into her journal, and she prayed that God would free her from bondage to the idols of profession, reputation, and friends.

*August 17, 1975, Sunday*

*The day of the Lord is coming when many who have disowned Me will find themselves in great darkness. There is no true security except in Me, no true peace except in My Peace. The world of evil will not hear My call, but you are sons and daughters of Light. Be sober and vigilant against the deceitful wiles of the enemy. Be centered in Me—not in other human beings. Beware of IDOLATRY OF HUMANS.*

In the midst of her Sunday morning rhythm, there came a knock at the door: Arlene was needed in the O.B. ward. She immediately knew she was either going to be late for church or unable to attend at all. But the birth went quickly, and Arlene decided to walk across the mountain, knowing that the service would be long and worthwhile even if she arrived in time for only a portion. She did arrive for the last part of the service. Her homeward walk was interrupted by two Jehovah's Witnesses who gave her a tract and asked for a conversation. Arlene told them where she lived and said that she was always eager to talk about Jesus. They said they would come by, but Arlene's journal doesn't record that they ever did.

## ✚ Questions for Reflection/Discussion

1. Arlene identified "profession, reputation, and friends" as her potential idols. What are yours?

2. Mother Basilea helped Arlene remain centered in Jesus. Who is someone you look up to who redirects your gaze to Jesus?

3. Have you recently had a conversation with someone about Jesus?

 *Message 17*

This book of the law shall not depart out of your mouth, but you shall meditate on it day and night, that you may be careful to do according to all that is written in it; for then you shall make your way prosperous, and then you shall have good success. Have I not commanded you? Be strong and of good courage; be not frightened, neither be dismayed; for the LORD your God is with you wherever you go.

Joshua 1:8–9 (RSV)

On Monday, the friend of Arlene's accuser came to see her. She was glad they could now speak easily with each other, and she invited him to stay for dinner. After dinner, he admitted that he had a request for Arlene. He had become convinced that a friend of hers was not an authentic Christian, but rather a liar and a thief. He asked Arlene to stop supporting this man, to stop being his friend.

By now, it was nearly midnight. Arlene had listened, and now it was her turn to speak. She chose her words carefully and didn't reveal her full heart. She said that the man they were speaking of did not have to answer to her but to the Lord and that she would continue to respect him as a Christian brother. She would leave it at that, she said, and she wanted to avoid taking a side in the debate between the elders and the accusers.

But her words hid a deep struggle that had occurred. This was the very man about whom she had confessed jealousy several months earlier. Her relationship with him had never become romantic or physically inappropriate, but he was the most faithful and understanding of all her Ethiopian friends. She had loved him as a dear friend, but she had quietly stepped away from the friendship because of her own jealousy. Arlene wanted to ensure that nothing ever stood in the way between her and her God. She was a woman called to a single allegiance, and she had written her intentions in the following prayer back in January:

*I bring You no oblation or sacrifice, my God,*
*only a foolish and self-centered heart.*

*I do come to You with a sincere desire to be Your Servant:*
*to walk in Your course for my life,*
*to receive Your love, and to channel such love to my fellow man*
*about me.*

*I thank You, God, that this is acceptable to You and that I will*
*remain Your daughter forever!*

<u>*My goal*</u>*: The marriage Supper of the Lamb.*

<u>*My need*</u>*: True bridal love toward Jesus.*

<u>*My request*</u>*: Show me what it involves—I AM WILLING EVEN*
*TO THE SHEDDING OF BLOOD.*

Her accuser's friend said goodnight. They parted amicably. But before she laid her head on her pillow, she wrote of their meeting. Then sometime in the early morning hours as the earth turned from Monday into Tuesday, she recorded a message that confirmed her own desire.

*August 19, 1975, Tuesday*

*Do not let a spirit of idolatry mislead you into sin. When you make a god of a human being, you lay yourself open to Satan's trap: <u>he can deceive you through another person's weakness</u>! No one is infallible. Be conformed to My Word, not to other people's standards or personalities or interpretation of My Word. Seek the gift of discernment of My Holy Spirit to lead you into all truth. Test this in my Word.*

*You have mourned for a lost love. Let me comfort you with My Love. Let me give you a garland, the mantle of praise, and the oil of gladness—that I may be glorified.*

## ✠ Questions for Reflection/Discussion

1. "You shall meditate on it day and night," says Joshua, speaking of the law of God. What do you meditate on day and night?

2. Arlene's persistent goal was to attend "the marriage Supper of the Lamb." Imagine attending that feast and then describe it.

3. Who is someone you know who wears "a garland, the mantle of praise, and the oil of gladness," and what is it like to be in the presence of that person?

# ✚ Message 18

Thus says the LORD:
Heaven is my throne
   and the earth is my footstool;
so what kind of house could you build for me,
   what sort of place for me to rest?
All these things my hand has made,
   and so all these things are mine, says the LORD.
But this is the one to whom I will look,
   to the humble and contrite in spirit,
   who trembles at my word.

Isaiah 66:1–2 (NRSVue)

One Tuesday, Arlene reported in her journal that she had completed an errand:

*Went to see Mister Hussein, Administrator, about Harvey's request to build office at Teppi.*

There was a great deal behind that single sentence. The administrative offices for the Illuabor province were in Mettu, and so a person from Teppi who wanted a building permit was required to fill out a form in person in Mettu. But Teppi was a hundred miles away, and travel on the mountain roads could take days—depending on the weather, road maintenance, and government check points. It was therefore reasonable that a Teppi person would radio a Mettu person and ask them to go to the provincial office on their behalf. On this occasion, the Mettu person receiving the radio request was Arlene.

Arlene couldn't know that in a little more than a year, everyone at both the Mettu and Teppi missions would be sent out of the country. But the morning after her errand to the provincial administrator, her message from the Lord reminded her that neither the missionaries nor the Ethiopians were ultimately in control.

*August 20, 1975, Wednesday*

> *Do not pride yourself on your fine churches and sanctuaries,*
> *for heaven is My throne. The earth is only My footstool. I am*
> *not impressed by human titles or accomplishments, but <u>I seek</u>*
> *<u>out</u> <u>the</u> <u>one</u> <u>who</u> <u>is</u> <u>humble</u> and <u>contrite</u> <u>in</u> <u>heart</u> <u>who</u> <u>obeys</u> <u>My</u>*
> *<u>Word</u>. That is the one whom I will use mightily!*

## ✚ Questions for Reflection/Discussion

1. In what ways did Harvey's request require Arlene to humble herself?

2. "All these things are mine, says the Lord." What are a few things, large and small, of which you can say today, "All these things God's hand has made"?

3. What strategies do you have for being pleased with your work while at the same time avoiding the sin of pride?

## ✚ *Message 19*

You made all the delicate, inner parts of my body
and knit me together in my mother's womb.
Thank you for making me so wonderfully complex!
Your workmanship is marvelous—how well I know it.
You watched me as I was being formed in utter seclusion,
as I was woven together in the dark of the womb.
You saw me before I was born.
Every day of my life was recorded in your book.
Every moment was laid out
before a single day had passed.

Psalm 139:13–16 (NLT)

The first thing Arlene wrote in her journal on August 22 was *Mom's 78th birthday*. Arlene knew that her family, who planned and accomplished nearly everything early, had already celebrated Johanna Rozeboom Schuiteman's birthday. The *Sioux Center News* even carried a brief description of the event. In keeping with the conventions of the time, almost all of the women's names were subsumed within the names of their husbands.

Mrs. John G. Schuiteman was guest of honor at a family dinner party held at the Holland House Thursday evening, August 7, for her 78th birthday which will be August 22. Children and grandchildren attended.

Present, besides Mrs. Schuiteman and Grada, were Mr. and Mrs. Henry Boterhoek and daughters, Sheldon; Mr. and Mrs. Howard Sandbulte and children, Sioux Center; Rev. and Mrs. Wilmer Ver Meer and sons, Hollandale, Minn.; and Mr. and Mrs. Lee Ten Brink and children of Holland, Mich.

Grada was the only female name in the article, but this was because she was unmarried. Arlene's other sisters (Harriet, Bernice, Joyce, and Milly) were listed in the article only as "Mrs.," which was in keeping with formal print of the era. Arlene was sometimes included by saying, "another daughter, Arlene, who serves as a missionary nurse on the African continent," but on this occasion she was left out of the family reckoning. It was one of a thousand small cuts Arlene had long ago accepted. Then came today's whisper from the Lord, affirming his call on her life.

*August 22, 1975, Friday*

> *Before you were formed in the womb, you were called to serve Me. I have appointed you to be a prophet, and you shall speak My Words to all to whom I send you. Listen carefully for My still, small voice. Be not afraid to speak whatever words I command you, for I will protect you and deliver you. Do not go ahead of Me. Wait upon My Spirit to move your lips. Wait upon Me with prayer and fasting; in praise and thanksgiving let your requests be made known to Me.*

> *Be not afraid of the <u>new</u> way I am preparing for you. My cup will be a cup of blessing, filled and running over. With the mercy you show to others you will receive mercy. Be strong in My strength. Go forth in courage to be My instrument of grace to those in need. Trust only in Me. Go, for I am with you—wherever you go, I will be with you.*

## ✚ Questions for Reflection/Discussion

1. How has Arlene honored her mother?

2. What disappointments have you experienced in the past few days? What joys?

3. What new way is God preparing for you at this time in your life?

# ✚ *Message 20*

Long ago the LORD said to Israel:
"I have loved you, my people, with an everlasting love.
   With unfailing love I have drawn you to myself.
I will rebuild you, my virgin Israel.
   You will again be happy
   and dance merrily with your tambourines.
Again you will plant your vineyards on the mountains of Samaria
   and eat from your own gardens there."

Jeremiah 31:3–5 (NLT)

---

It seemed to Arlene as if something was being rebuilt in her. Her joy returned as her struggles with her accuser were coming to an end. She felt ready to meet her accuser again in person, even though a few weeks earlier she had admitted to the Lord that she never wanted to see him again. Now she hoped he would return so that the work of reconciliation could come to completion.

Whether her accuser returned or not, however, it seemed to her that God was using the accusations as part of his answer to her prayer from eight months earlier. She had prayed, *Show me what it involves*—that is, to show true love toward Jesus. Now she sat with her devotional guide, open Bible, and the small black journal with the red binding on the spine, and she received a brief message from the Lord indicating that these past months had indeed meant something.

*August 23, 1975, Saturday*

*You have turned back to Me now at last. Make your commitment to Me a vow that will keep you in Thanksgiving not out of duty. Delight to call upon Me. Want to glorify Me, more than yourself.*

## ✚ *Questions for Reflection/Discussion*

1. "You will again be happy," said the Lord to the people of Israel. When were some times of sadness in your personal life, church life, or civic life that eventually turned to joy?

2. When have you prayed in some way similar to Arlene's prayer, "Show me what it involves to show true love toward Jesus"?

3. Consider the action points within Message 20: Turn back to me, make a vow, delight to call, want to glorify. Do any of these beckon to you? If so, why?

# ✛ *Message 21*

"It is like a man going on a journey, when he leaves home and puts his servants in charge, each with his work, and commands the door-keeper to be on the watch. Watch therefore—for you do not know when the master of the house will come, in the evening, or at midnight, or at cockcrow, or in the morning—lest he come suddenly and find you asleep. And what I say to you I say to all: Watch."

Mark 13:34–37 (TLB)

Early in the morning in the middle of the next week, Arlene recorded her twenty-first message from the Lord—which began as an echo of the words of the ancient prophet Isaiah,

*For as the heavens are higher than the earth, so are my ways higher than your ways, and my thoughts than your thoughts.*

After this biblical beginning, Arlene's message took a turn, and by its ending, referred not generally to "your ways" and "your thoughts" but specifically to "this relationship." The Lord was whispering a promise to provide for her request of reconciliation with her accuser.

*August 27, 1975, Wednesday*

*Do not be disturbed that things are not as you planned, My child. My ways are not your ways. My thoughts are higher than your thoughts. My miracles often come about silently in the heart before they are seen by others. Be patient. Continue <u>perseveringly</u> in prayer. Keep your spirits high in praise and thanksgiving. <u>Wait upon Me to bring forth My answer of healing in this relationship</u>.*

Understanding what the prophecy meant, she wrote,

*Jesus, Precious Jesus—thank you—*

She didn't have to wait long. A friend arrived later that very day from down by the river at Gambela, carrying the much-anticipated letter from her accuser. After reading it, she wrote in her journal,

*An Apology. What a day!!!*

## ✚ Questions for Reflection/Discussion

1. What might Arlene have identified as the miracles of this day?

2. When did someone apologize to you, and what was the result?

3. What's something about which you prayed "perseveringly"?

# ✚ *Message 22*

Rejoice in the Lord always; again I will say, Rejoice. Let your gentleness be known to everyone. The Lord is near. Do not be anxious about anything, but in everything by prayer and supplication with thanksgiving let your requests be made known to God. And the peace of God, which surpasses all understanding, will guard your hearts and your minds in Christ Jesus.

Finally, brothers and sisters, whatever is true, whatever is honorable, whatever is just, whatever is pure, whatever is pleasing, whatever is commendable, if there is any excellence and if there is anything worthy of praise, think about these things. As for the things that you have learned and received and heard and noticed in me, do them, and the God of peace will be with you.

Philippians 4:4–9 (NRSVue)

Arlene climbed out of bed on Friday wondering how she would stay awake that day and whether she should write a letter of response to her accuser. That morning's message from the Lord addressed both questions.

*August 29, 1975, Friday*

*When you become tense, rest in Me. AT ONCE. Do not dally with thoughts of weariness and self-pity. Do not criticize others or become impatient with them. Ask for and claim My Patience—My supply for all your needs. I am concerned with all the details of your life. You need not be anxious if you stop at once to open the windows of your spirit to the flooding of My Love.*

Arlene's busy day at the hospital and school included planning that year's graduation program. Then after work, she walked in the rain to a friend's house for coffee. She wasn't hungry for supper when she arrived back home, so she picked up a sheet of white paper and fed it into her typewriter. She centered the carriage at the top of the page and typed, *CONFIDENTIAL*. It was 9:00 p.m. when she started writing *Dear friend and Christian Brother* to her accuser. The letter would eventually run three pages, single spaced, and read (in part):

> *I had hoped to see you and talk with you. However, I want you to hear that I forgive you* <u>*completely*</u> *and* <u>*forever*</u>.
>
> *I can even say thank you for writing, and I believe God used this experience to answer a prayer I prayed on December 18th, at a time when God was very close to me. It was shortly after that when I was convicted of jealousy, lust, critical tongue, self-righteousness, and pride. I confessed, repented, and was forgiven. It takes only a few lines to write that statement but you can see that it is loaded and not a simple unimportant event. In some cases, this involved apologies to individuals.*
>
> *I thank you for all the horrible, shocking statements you made concerning my relationship with a male friend. Mostly because it came as a warning of the danger that any close friendship can, in subtle ways, become twisted or harmful rather than something good.*
>
> *It may be that you discern other areas of sin or weakness as you read THIS letter. If so, please be so kind as to tell me (kindly, if possible* [drawing of smiley face] *otherwise, harshly again* [drawing of weepy face]).
>
> *Your gullible, misguided, beguiled, easily deceived, BUT grateful friend for whom Christ died,*
>
> *Lovingly, Arlene*

Arlene sent the letter in care of friends in the church at Gambela, hoping it would be passed by hand to the recipient. Weeks later, the letter made its way back to her, unopened—*Return to Sender, Address Unknown*. The saga was complete.

## ✚ Questions for Reflection/Discussion

1. Paul commends us to "let your gentleness be known to everyone." Who are a few people you know who would be called "gentle" by nearly everyone who knows them?

2. Why do you think Message 22 is so urgent about responding to tension "_AT ONCE_"?

3. What did you find remarkable about Arlene's letter?

# ✚ *Message 23*

"For thus said the Lord GOD, the Holy One of Israel,
   'In returning and rest you shall be saved;
   in quietness and in trust shall be your strength.'"
                                             Isaiah 30:15 (RSV)

On the final day of *Nehasa*, the Ethiopian twelfth calendar month, the grumbling among Arlene's students grew to a climax. They had learned that they would not be paid for the month of *Pagomen*, the thirteenth and final month of the year. Since the first twelve months in Ethiopia are each thirty days long, the thirteenth month represents the five or six remaining days, depending on whether or not it's a leap year. In 1975, *Pagomen* was six days long, and New Year's Day (*Moskarum*) fell on September 12 of the Western calendar.

In addition to the bitterness of her students, Arlene had a bad cold. Her nose dripped for days, and her strength was gone. Nevertheless, she kept up her routines of daily devotions, journal writing, and reading. That week, a missionary friend named Breezy overnighted with Arlene on her way from Germany back to her work in Africa. Breezy had been to the retreat center at the Evangelical Sisterhood of Mary. Hearing of their work was a balm to Arlene's spirit and an affirmation of her own pursuit of loving Jesus with her whole heart.

In the meantime, local trouble was still brewing. Arlene knew that the disgruntlement of her students would likely evidence itself fully on September 5, the last day of *Nehasa*. That morning, before heading off to the school, she received this message from the Lord.

*September 5, 1975, Friday*

> *My daughter, you have been under many pressures. Rest now in Me and let My Love renew your spirit. In quiet contemplation let My Spirit lead your spirit into new depths of Wisdom. You have been giving out much. Let Me now refill you. Enter into My silence—and rest. Rest in Me.*

Arlene spread the word at school that she wanted to meet with the students the next morning at 8:00 a.m.—the first day of the short month of *Pagomen*.

## Questions for Reflection/Discussion

1. Why is sleep so important?

2. When have you experienced lengthy times of silence? How did it make you feel?

3. If you're feeling anxious today, why?

# ✠ *Message 24*

For God is so wise and so mighty.
    Who has ever challenged him successfully?
Without warning, he moves the mountains,
    overturning them in his anger.
He shakes the earth from its place,
    and its foundations tremble.
If he commands it, the sun won't rise
    and the stars won't shine.
He alone has spread out the heavens
    and marches on the waves of the sea.

Job 9:4–8 (NLT)

Arlene's first thought on Saturday morning was that she should stay home. She felt sick. She was sick. But she put on her uniform, walked to the school, and waited for her students as she said she would. They straggled in late, looking glum, expecting to be told they would not be paid for *Pagomen*, expecting to go on strike the next week.

Arlene loved her students, but she believed that they needed her to take a firm position. She wrote in her journal what she planned to say:

1. *You will continue to receive your usual stipend through graduation day.*

2. *Your work stipend is based on the twelve months of the European calendar. You are already being paid for the six days of Pagomen. It would not be right to pay you twice for those days.*

3. *You do not make the school rules.*

4. *You have known the rules and promised to keep them.*

5. *Your class has had a posture of complaint. The staff and I are fed up. You may leave if you wish.*

6. *Your own attitude will be represented in any recommendation I write on your behalf.*

7. *Remember that you do not yet have the results of your national exam.*

Although Arlene didn't report in her journal what happened at the meeting that morning, the students didn't go on strike the following week.

She went to bed early that night but shortly after midnight was asked to come to the O.B. ward. She made an uncharacteristic decision not to go. Others would have to manage in her place. God had told her to rest. She stayed home from church on Sunday. At the end of the day, she recorded this message in her journal.

*September 7, 1975, Sunday*

*I have many purposes for the days ahead. <u>Some</u> of them will be <u>dark days</u>. <u>Some</u> will be stormy—but be not afraid. My peace will abide in you in the midst of storms. You will be lifted over the waves. You will be carried through the darkness in Light that no one can quench. You have <u>nothing</u> to <u>fear</u>. Your faith will be strengthened in My Presence. <u>Do</u> <u>not</u> <u>let</u> <u>your</u> <u>fears</u> <u>rock</u> <u>the</u> <u>boat</u>. <u>Be</u> <u>still</u> <u>and</u> <u>know!</u>*

## ✠ Questions for Reflection/Discussion

1. If you had been one of Arlene's students that day, would you have gone on strike? Why or why not?

2. When have you been called on to diffuse a conflict? What did you do?

3. Are there any ways the Lord may be preparing you for dark days ahead?

 *Message 25*

So Samuel did as the LORD instructed. When he arrived at Bethlehem, the elders of the town came trembling to meet him. "What's wrong?" they asked. "Do you come in peace?"

"Yes," Samuel replied. "I have come to sacrifice to the LORD. Purify yourselves and come with me to the sacrifice." Then Samuel performed the purification rite for Jesse and his sons and invited them to the sacrifice, too.

When they arrived, Samuel took one look at Eliab and thought, "Surely this is the LORD's anointed!"

But the LORD said to Samuel, "Don't judge by his appearance or height, for I have rejected him. The LORD doesn't see things the way you see them. People judge by outward appearance, but the LORD looks at the heart."

1 Samuel 16:4–7 (NLT)

Arlene listened often to the cassette tapes of British preacher Derek Prince's sermons. Today's sermon was on worship. She took careful notes, and then she reexamined the message from the Lord she had written at the end of the previous day. She took the prophecy seriously:

*I have many purposes for the days ahead. Some of them will be dark days. Some will be stormy.*

Arlene prepared herself by praying,

*I want You to cleanse and control the very depths of my mind, heart, and desires.*

She sensed a new adventure in the Spirit, and the following prophecy confirmed it.

*September 8, 1975, Monday*

> *The new doorway that I am opening is not an easy one, but it will be rewarding. In the Spirit you will be led into deeper intercessions for those in need. I will teach you much that you have never learned, but it will not be for yourself alone. I know your innermost thoughts. You need only to pray to be kept in the center of My highest Will for your life.*

Her cold persisted, but she went to work anyway. By evening, she was exhausted and went to bed at 8:00 p.m.

---

## ✚ Questions for Reflection/Discussion

1. What is a circumstance when you, like Samuel, judged wrongly because you were evaluating by appearance rather than by what is unseen?

2. What are some ways you can prepare spiritually without knowing specifically what you're preparing for?

3. When might preparation become an obstacle to faith?

 *Message 26*

For "Everyone who calls on the name of the LORD will be saved." But how can they call on him to save them unless they believe in him? And how can they believe in him if they have never heard about him? And how can they hear about him unless someone tells them? And how will anyone go and tell them without being sent? That is why the Scriptures say, "How beautiful are the feet of messengers who bring good news!"

Romans 10:13–15 (NLT)

Arlene awoke the next morning with the memory of a dream. She was on an island. Her mission director, Harold Kurtz, was the only other person there. He was about to leave her alone on the island, asking her if she was sure she wanted to stay—she might be cut off from all communications. She stayed. Then a boat came by offering one final chance to leave the island. Bombs began falling all around. If she was going to leave, she needed to go now. She stayed. And then she woke up.

Something was afoot. She was being prepared for something. Was it the Lord preparing her? Or were her private fears nattering at her in the typical way that actors have dreams before major performances and teachers have dreams at the start of a new semester?

With graduation only a week and a half away, she was coming to the end of one cohort, waiting to find out if her students had passed their national exams, and preparing to receive the new cohort in a few weeks. Or was it the continuing changes of the revolutionary government with its threats of violence?

Arlene wrote down a description of the dream but didn't attempt an interpretation. Then she received this message.

*September 9, 1975, Tuesday*

> *I have new plans for your life. Some are beyond your furtherest hopes. In obedient trust they will be fulfilled—but not by striving or straining. Let Me bring these opportunities for service in My timing. Be open. Be receptive. Be loving. Be expectant. Do joyously whatever I give you to do, no matter how small. Be My message to those about you.*

## ✠ Questions for Reflection/Discussion

1. When Paul wrote his letter to the Roman church, he was alluding to Isaiah, which says, "How beautiful on the mountains are the feet of the messenger who brings good news." What makes those feet beautiful?

2. When have dreams in the Bible carried special meaning?

3. How did Message 26 connect with Arlene's dream?

 *Message 27*

The LORD is merciful and gracious,
    slow to anger and abounding in steadfast love.
He will not always chide,
    nor will he keep his anger for ever.
He does not deal with us according to our sins,
    nor requite us according to our iniquities.
For as the heavens are high above the earth,
    so great is his steadfast love toward those who fear him;
as far as the east is from the west,
    so far does he remove our transgressions from us.
As a father pities his children,
    so the LORD pities those who fear him.
For he knows our frame;
    he remembers that we are dust.

Psalm 103: 8–14 (RSV)

Friday, September 12, was *Moskarum 1*—the first day of the first month of the new Ethiopian year. Arlene had been continuing to listen to Derek Prince sermon tapes, specifically about Old Testament worship rituals. At the start of this new year, while thinking of Leviticus 4, she wrote down prayers for cleansing:

*Jesus my altar for sin offering:*

    *1. Cleanse away pockets of infection (cold, etc.)*

    *2. Cleanse away dullness of mind*

    *3. Cleanse away lethargy*

    *4. Cleanse away my desire for honor or praise from people*

    *5. Cleanse away the self-deception, self-love*

    *6. Cleanse away reluctance to bear my cross*

Although it was a national holiday, Arlene didn't attend any celebrations. Instead, she cleaned her soul and her stencil cupboard.

That afternoon, she listened to the news via the R.T. (radio telephone). The BBC reported that the Ethiopian government announced *Moskarum 2* as a new holiday—Revolution Day, chosen because it was the one-year anniversary of the deposing of Emperor Haile Selassie. The day was to be marked by the execution of twelve of the royal family along with eighteen others. America and several European countries announced their outrage.

On Saturday, Arlene walked to the football stadium to observe the Revolution Day activities where there was a parade with two floats. There was a government edict that all residents of Mettu were to return to the football field the next morning for announcements. Since Arlene had grown up in a community that supported Sunday as a day set aside for worship, she received the government's dictum as an affront to the church.

*September 14, 1975, Sunday*

> *In the fire of My Holiness, your sins have been consumed, My child. You have repented and asked My forgiveness. Accept My Joy through sins forgiven. Accept My grace to go and sin no more. I have purified your heart. No more shall you hold these secret guilts. They are washed away in the Blood of the Lamb. I am glorified in your joy as you go in praise and thanksgiving. Show forth My Praise.*

> *Because you love Me, you hate this evil attack that has come upon your church. The enemy <u>cannot</u> prevail against those who love Me. Claim the delivering Power of My Blood. You hate the evil, but you must not hate the sinner. Pray against the devil's attack, but pray for deliverance of those who have allowed themselves to become his minions. I am preserving you from the hands of the ungodly. Rejoice!*

After recording the above message, Arlene walked to the football stadium for the announcements. She wondered how the event would interfere with morning worship, but the government's event was over in an hour. She walked to church and found an unusually large crowd who simply wouldn't stop worshiping. She also reported that several people were healed during the prayers at the end of the worship service.

 *Questions for Reflection/Discussion*

1. Arlene's church clearly believed in miraculous healing. When have you prayed for healing or experienced a Christian gathering in which healings occurred?

2. What museums have you visited that told the stories of violence in times of human struggle?

3. Message 27 promised that Arlene would be preserved "from the hands of the ungodly." Can you think of times when believers have not been preserved from violence?

# ✚ *Message 28*

The LORD is my shepherd; I shall not want.
    He maketh me to lie down in green pastures:
he leadeth me beside the still waters.
    He restoreth my soul:
he leadeth me in the paths of righteousness
      for his name's sake.
Yea, though I walk through the valley of the shadow of death,
    I will fear no evil:
for thou art with me;
      thy rod and thy staff
        they comfort me.
Thou preparest a table before me
    in the presence of mine enemies:
thou anointest my head with oil;
      my cup runneth over.
Surely goodness and mercy shall follow me
    all the days of my life:
and I will dwell in the house of the LORD
      for ever.

Psalm 23 (KJV)

Graduation was scheduled for Thursday. Arlene had selected a small alarm clock as a gift for each student, and she had purchased a sheep for the graduation feast. But the Ministry of Public Health had not yet announced the scores of the national exams, and her students said they didn't want a feast until they were certain they had passed the national exam.

*September 17, 1975, Wednesday*

*My child, I have loved you with an everlasting love, and I have appointed you to bear much fruit. Fear not to go forth and do the works I have called you to do. The enemy has assaulted you through your loved ones, and you have nothing to fear. My <u>rod</u> and My <u>staff</u> strengthen you. I shall spread a table before you in the presence of your enemies. Your cup shall run over with*

*My Joy. Goodness and mercy shall flow out of you, and you shall dwell in My Presence all the days of your life.*

The day ended with no word from the Ministry of Public Health concerning the exams. Although it rained all day, the clouds cleared at sunset. As sparkling water dripped from the leaves of her frangipani bush, Arlene noted in her journal that it was gorgeous. That evening, she received that day's second message from the Lord.

*I have set you in a watered garden where beauty abounds so that your spirit may be refreshed by My creation! Accept <u>all</u> I have given you in praise and thanksgiving, for My heart delights to give good gifts to My children. The sun shines on the just and on the unjust, <u>but</u> the bounty of My Love is reserved for those who, in obedience, abide in My Will. You have been faithful in little things, <u>and</u> <u>I</u> <u>shall</u> <u>add</u> <u>more</u> <u>to</u> <u>them.</u> <u>Be</u> <u>faithful</u> <u>also</u> <u>in</u> <u>much</u>.*

## ✚ Questions for Reflection/Discussion

1. What does Psalm 23 mean in your life?

2. In what ways has God borne fruit through you?

3. When has God ministered to you through creation?

# ✚ *Message 29*

And I am convinced that nothing can ever separate us from God's love. Neither death nor life, neither angels nor demons, neither our fears for today nor our worries about tomorrow—not even the powers of hell can separate us from God's love. No power in the sky above or in the earth below—indeed, nothing in all creation will ever be able to separate us from the love of God that is revealed in Christ Jesus our Lord.

Romans 8:38–39 (NLT)

At noon on Mettu Dresser School's 1975 graduation day, the R.T. crackled to life. "Three-Nine, Three-Nine, do you read? All your students have passed the national exam. Repeat, all students have passed." There would indeed be feasting in Mettu! Later, Arlene would learn the specifics. One of her eleven graduates earned the highest score in the nation and another earned the third highest score. Her school had been successful in an especially difficult year due to a challenging schedule brought on by changes in the government. Only two other schools in the nation had all passes, and one school had seen a third of its students fail.

Early Sunday morning, Arlene resumed her practice of examining herself for any evidence of sin. Today, she laid before the Lord her pride that all her students had passed the national exam. She also begged God for personal sanctification in a list worthy of a Christian's daily repetition:

1. *Give me a good heart.*

2. *Help me love You more—stretch and strengthen my heart; stimulate my powers of concentration on You.*

3. *Bend all my energy to do Thy Will!*

4. *Help me differentiate between my selfish desires and Your pure Will.*

Then her prayers turned to her students—those just graduated and those soon arriving. She listed family, friends, and colleagues—dozens of people near and far. Then before setting her journal aside so she could walk to worship, she recorded a message from the Lord—the most specific message she had yet received.

*September 21, 1975, Sunday*

> *I need you today on a special errand of mercy. There is one who has not been able to hear My Words of Love, My Good News. She is one who is defeated by memories of the battles of the past. She cannot set herself free. She cannot hear My Voice. She does not understand the Good News of My Love that will redeem the past. Be My Forgiving Love to her this day. Be My hand extended. Let Me touch her through you in mercy.*

Sadly, none of Arlene's journals and letters reveal the identity of the woman mentioned. Then again, was the message so specific after all? Is there ever a day when the Lord doesn't say to his disciples: *I need you to go on an errand of mercy—to one who needs to hear my words of love, my good news.*

## ✛ Questions for Reflection/Discussion

1. Which of your teachers taught you the value of celebration?

2. To whom has the Lord recently sent you on an errand of mercy?

3. How do you respond to Arlene's four-part prayer of sanctification? Is it a prayer you would feel comfortable praying?

 *Message 30*

> Put on then, as God's chosen ones, holy and beloved, compassion, kindness, lowliness, meekness, and patience, forbearing one another and, if one has a complaint against another, forgiving each other; as the Lord has forgiven you, so you also must forgive.
>
> Colossians 3:12–13 (RSV)

Arlene caught the bus to the capital city—a fourteen-hour trip that started at 5:00 a.m. She took the school's mimeograph machine with her to get it overhauled, but the office supply store said it would take three days. When one lives fourteen hours from town, one is willing to wait three days.

She spent those days going carefully down a shopping list for herself and many others. After three days, the machine was ready and Arlene was back on the bus headed west. It was an old bus with a young driver—a troublesome combination on any road in any country. Going up each grade in that mountainous region, the bus slowed and chugged. Finally, at 9:30 that night, the engine quit altogether. All the passengers exited and searched for somewhere to sleep. A kind gentleman secured a bed for "the middle-aged, White lady." Although Arlene turned out to be sharing the bed with some biting bugs, she was exhausted enough to get some sleep. Thirty hours after the trip had begun, the bus limped into Mettu.

The next day was full of activity. In her morning journaling, Arlene wrote,

> *Today I want to experience the purpose for which I was created—to worship the Triune God and have fellowship with Him, spirit to Spirit.*

The church building overflowed, with some fifty people left standing during the three-hour service. One woman was delivered of a demon.

That day was one of Ethiopia's most important religious holidays. Some children in Arlene's neighborhood invited her to come with them to the *Meskel* (Cross) bonfire in memory of Saint Helena's fourth-century discovery of the cross on which Jesus died. The tale of Helena's find is a miraculous story involving a bonfire and smoke that guided her to the place of the cross. That was, of course, a great moment for relic hunters. A piece of the artifact resides at the Gishen Mariam monastery, three hundred miles north of Addis Ababa.

*September 29, 1975, Monday*

> *Rest in Me now for your labors have been arduous. Rest beside the still waters. I have brought you through a situation of turmoil, and the storm has now abated. Rest in Me as I set you in green pastures. Let Me anoint your head with the oil of My Joy. Let Me fill you to overflowing with My Refreshing Love. Let Me renew your spirit now.*

## ✚ Questions for Reflection/Discussion

1. How would you compare Arlene's perspective on worship to your own?

2. Do you think that religious relics are helps or hindrances to faith?

3. Did a delay ever become a blessing to you?

# ✚ *Message 31*

But he knows every detail of what is happening to me; and when he has examined me, he will pronounce me completely innocent—as pure as solid gold!

I have stayed in God's paths, following his steps. I have not turned aside. I have not refused his commandments but have enjoyed them more than my daily food. Nevertheless, his mind concerning me remains unchanged, and who can turn him from his purposes? Whatever he wants to do, he does. So he will do to me all he has planned, and there is more ahead.

Job 23:10–14 (TLB)

The government had told Arlene to delay the start of school by a month because they were considering making changes. On this day, a young man arrived after walking all the way from Teppi—about a hundred miles away!—hoping to start his studies at the dresser school that week. He hadn't received the news that school was delayed, and Arlene set about finding him a place to stay.

What was God's intent for the school with its uncertain schedule, for the church with its standing room only, for the hospital with its alcoholic doctor, for the nation with its gasoline shortages, floundering government, and massive swaths of starving people? Arlene had been raised in a church that valued reading and singing the biblical psalms, including the psalms of lament. She would need those on a day like today, when the Derg government declared that the capital city was under martial law.

*September 30, 1975, Tuesday*

> *This mission is an important one, although it may not seem so to you. Lift it to Me now. Release it to Me, every detail. Know that I will be within you—in the midst of this gathering. I will be present <u>in Love</u> and <u>in Power</u> <u>to teach</u> and <u>to heal</u> and <u>to bless</u>.*

## ✠ Questions for Reflection/Discussion

1. Who is someone you know about whom you can imagine saying, "That person is as pure as solid gold"?

2. What would you do if you discovered that the only available doctor in your hospital was an untreated alcoholic?

3. What are the advantages of praying the psalms of lament?

## Message 32

What agreement has the temple of God with idols? For we are the
temple of the living God; as God said,

> "I will live in them and move among them,
> and I will be their God,
> and they shall be my people.
> Therefore come out from them,
> and be separate from them, says the Lord,
> and touch nothing unclean;
> then I will welcome you,
> and I will be a father to you,
> and you shall be my sons and daughters,
> says the Lord Almighty."

Since we have these promises, beloved, let us cleanse ourselves from
every defilement of body and spirit, and make holiness perfect in
the fear of God.

2 Corinthians 6:16–18; 7:1 (RSV)

Arlene had studied the spiritual importance of fasting. She had
completed several fasts, including a five-day fast. But it was now
nine months since she had practiced this spiritual discipline. She
felt it was time to resume the practice, starting with a two-day fast.
On the first day of the fast, she felt aches and nausea. She wondered
if she was coming down with the flu or feeling the results of the
fasting. She wrote in her journal:

*We have nothing of our own but our will. It is of this which
God is jealous. He has given it to us—to give back to him.*

Arlene confessed in her journal that she was struggling with
pride over her students' exam scores. She also admitted that she was
lethargic in not starting her morning prayers in a timely manner.
Then she recorded the following message:

*October 4, 1975, Saturday*

> <u>Beloved</u>, <u>you</u> are the temple of My Holy Spirit. Do not willfully defile My temple. You have a great part to play in the cleansing of the temple, for I will not overrule your freedom of will. You must make holiness your aim. You must by an act of will cleanse yourself from the habits that defile our body—gluttony is one of them. Do not expose yourself to the old temptations, but replace them with greater love for Me. Take My hand for I am your Father. You cannot do this cleansing alone, but I cannot do it without your surrender of will! You must WANT to be Mine more than to lean on the old crutches, the old defiling habits.

## ✛ Questions for Reflection/Discussion

1. Where do you see idols in contemporary culture?

2. Have you ever fasted? If so, what was your experience and how would you describe its value?

3. In what ways do you treat your body like the temple of the Holy Spirit?

# ✚ *Message 33*

But, O my soul, don't be discouraged. Don't be upset. Expect God to act! For I know that I shall again have plenty of reason to praise him for all that he will do. He is my help! He is my God!

Psalm 42:11 (TLB)

The next day, even in her weakened state (whether from illness or fasting), Arlene didn't want to miss worship. She walked across the mountain to the church building. As she arrived, she saw the crowd clustered outside, trying to get a glimpse through the side openings. She knew she was in no shape to stand today, and not wanting to ask for someone's seat, she turned around and went home.

*October 5, 1975, Sunday*

*In your work with others do not try to argue. For the enemy loves to create dissension, and he will try to blind their minds with half-truths. Wait in quietness upon Me and let Me speak through you the words that will cut through their secret bondages. Let the Word of God be spoken through your lips. Be the Light to illumine the murky shadows in their hearts. You will be amazed to see their response. I need your voice to proclaim My good news in their special needs. Take none of the glory to yourself.*

She prayed in her journal,

*God uproot from my heart all that I want to plant there myself. Please plant there the tree of Life loaded with fruit.*

At the end of the day, her final note was:

*16 years ago that my Father died.*

## ✚ Questions for Reflection/Discussion

1. Arlene walked across the mountain to church only to turn around and go home. Did you ever have to leave a worship service because there wasn't enough room for you?

2. The message told Arlene to meet half-truths with silence. Why is this such a difficult assignment?

3. Who in your life was so special that every year you remember the anniversary of their death?

# ✚ Message 34

I will bless the LORD at all times;
  his praise shall continually be in my mouth.
My soul makes its boast in the LORD;
  let the afflicted hear and be glad.
O magnify the LORD with me,
  and let us exalt his name together!
I sought the LORD, and he answered me,
  and delivered me from all my fears.

Psalm 34:1–4 (RSV)

Iteffe's mother had been admitted to the Mettu hospital. An evangelist and pastor, Iteffe was one of the leaders in the revival that had spread in the western mountains five years earlier. He had been a good friend and guide to Arlene when she first began to speak in tongues. With such an experience so new and strange to someone of Arlene's background, he told her not to worry but to "praise God not for his gifts, but for who he is." He now lived and worked elsewhere, but he had visited a week earlier to see his mother.

After Iteffe left for home, his mother took a turn for the worse. The doctor had discovered a mass that would need surgery at a hospital in Addis Ababa. Arlene would need to try and get a message through to Iteffe.

*October 8, 1975, Wednesday*

*Look to me for <u>deliverance from your fears</u>, for My hand is not shortened today. The enemy is tempting the young to lead them astray, but My angels will be watching over those who want to be saved. As I delivered My servant David, so I can deliver your loved one today. Be steadfast in praise. Boast not in the accomplishments of people but in the mercy of God. <u>Sing praises</u> to the Name of the Lord whose mercy endures forever.*

## Questions for *Reflection/Discussion*

1. Have you ever needed to get a message to someone and didn't have a good way to do it?

2. If you were to boast about God, what are some of the first things you would say?

3. You probably attend worship at least once a week, and during that time you praise God. What other times during the week do you express your love, praise, and gratitude— either directly to God or to others about God?

## ✚ Message 35

Yet even now, says the LORD,
   return to me with all your heart,
with fasting, with weeping, and with mourning;
   rend your hearts and not your clothing.
Return to the LORD your God,
   for he is gracious and merciful,
slow to anger, and abounding in steadfast love,

                              Joel 2:12–13a (NRSVue)

The next morning, Arlene recorded a dream in her journal. In the dream, she was working down in Gambela among the Nuer; she had car trouble and lost her purse. After describing the dream, she recorded this message.

*October 9, 1975, Thursday*

> *You are My beloved. When you obey My commands, I am abiding within you to work out the details of your life. You need fear nothing but the loss of Me, for I can bring good out of evil and transform this situation. Turn each decision of your life over to Me so that I can fulfill My destiny for your life. I am working out your salvation but you must surrender your will to Me. Trust only in Me.*

What "evil" was the prophecy referring to? What "situation"? She wondered if the message was about Iteffe's mother. Arlene sent a telegram to Iteffe to come as soon as he could, telling him to prepare to transfer his mother to the city. When Arlene returned from sending the message, she checked the growth and discovered it had softened and begun to drain. When Iteffe arrived by bus that evening, his mother was greatly improved.

Perhaps the prophecy had been fulfilled by Iteffe's mother's healing, but Arlene was also aware of another "situation" that needed transforming. The government had still not provided a start date. She wrote in her journal:

*Worked in office on desk drawers and file. This break is very good for me in many ways. But if and when school will open remains cloaked in mystery.*

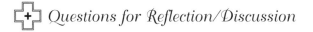 *Questions for Reflection/Discussion*

1. Do you resonate at all with Joel's description of weeping and mourning—a tearing not of clothing but of the heart? Can you recall a time when that's how you felt and, if so, what led to that depth of feeling?

2. What Bible stories come to mind in which a person was suddenly healed?

3. Who is a friend of yours whom you find especially trustworthy?

# ✚ *Message 36*

Then Mary, when she came where Jesus was and saw him, fell at his feet, saying to him, "Lord, if you had been here, my brother would not have died." When Jesus saw her weeping, and the Jews who came with her also weeping, he was deeply moved in spirit and troubled; and he said, "Where have you laid him?" They said to him, "Lord, come and see." Jesus wept. So the Jews said, "See how he loved him!" But some of them said, "Could not he who opened the eyes of the blind man have kept this man from dying?"

John 11:32–37 (RSV)

On Sunday afternoon, November 2, Arlene went to visit a former student. Back in 1967, he had been in her very first class at the Mettu Dresser School. He was one of the sweetest of her students; and shortly after her arrival, he had given her the gift of a small deerlike animal—a duiker. Arlene had named it Dikdik and, until it ran away into the forest, it had been a much-loved pet. Her student graduated and became a dresser. He married Wobitu, who became a member of the Mettu hospital staff. They had four children with one more on the way.

On Tuesday, October 21, Arlene had developed an upper respiratory infection. It was the beginning of a perfect storm. Several church leaders came over for conversation, and she was up much later than she wanted to be. She was awakened early the following morning to help with a breech delivery. Afterwards, she surprised the staff by telling them something they had never heard her say— she was going home and back to bed! At 4:00 that afternoon, she was called back to the O.B. ward. Wobitu was in active labor and in trouble. Arlene arrived to discover that it was a brow presentation, a serious dilemma. Arlene would later write,

*We had only two choices: 1) destruction of the fetus, or*
*2) Cesarean Section.*

Since there was no surgeon on site for the cesarean, Wobitu would have to be driven to a hospital five hours away. Arlene discerned that Wobitu was strong enough, and they laid her on a mattress in the back of the Land Rover. Wobitu made it only twenty miles. They called from Yayo to say that mother and baby had died on the way. In Ethiopia, burials happen within twenty-four hours of death. Arlene thought there were probably a thousand people at that funeral.

The next day in her journal, Arlene mulled over the circumstances. She felt that if she hadn't been sick in bed, she might have been able to admit Wobitu and make an earlier prognosis, possibly saving her life. The hospital was awash in tears all week.

Arlene took food to Wobitu's widower and their children. The following morning, the Lord spoke.

*November 3, 1975, Monday*

> *This one is being healed by My Love poured through you. When you feel impatient, ask Me for more of My Love in you. Take your eyes off the person and fix them on Me. Satan is attacking you and him with fear and doubts. You can claim the Power of My Blood over this situation now. Command this spirit of fear to <u>get</u> <u>out</u> <u>of you</u> in the Name of Jesus Christ. Claim My Love now to fill the pockets left vacant by the enemy. Put a circle of My purifying fire around you for protection. Now lift the person to Me again and let My love saturate him, filling every cell of his body. Think of him as immersed in My Love now.*

## ✚ Questions for Reflection/Discussion

1. If you had been Arlene experiencing the circumstances of Wobitu's death, do you think you might have blamed yourself?

2. When are fears or doubts a positive thing?

3. In Message 36, what actions did the Lord counsel Arlene to do?

# ✠ *Message 37*

See that none of you repays evil for evil, but always seek to do good
to one another and to all. Rejoice always, pray constantly, give thanks
in all circumstances; for this is the will of God in Christ Jesus for you.

1 Thessalonians 5:15–16 (RSV)

Even though the center of the revolutionary government was
in the capital city of Addis Ababa, the changes were being felt more
and more at Mettu. Ethiopia had long been a Christian nation, but
with the death of the emperor, it was becoming more secularized.
Although the government wasn't yet ready to stand against the Orthodox Church, the Derg's attitude toward Pentecostals was another story. Orthodox services began at sunrise and were over by
9:00 a.m. The government was therefore comfortable with setting
community meetings after nine on Sunday mornings, ignoring the
schedule of non-Orthodox worship.

One Sunday that fall, the police showed up at 9:30 at Arlene's
church and insisted that the worship service disband so everyone
could go and vote about something. After that, persons from the
Information Office began observing the church's Sunday gatherings.
Sometimes, young men from the town showed up to disrupt services. The elders at Arlene's church considered changing the time of
services to match the Orthodox Church, but they were concerned
that many people in their congregation walked from two to four
hours to get to worship, and such an early start would mean walking in the dark on mountain paths.

Some of Arlene's colleagues felt that the country's power had
fallen into hands that were too young, inexperienced, impetuous,
and violent. Arlene had witnessed the value of youthful passion
when wielded for the sake of the kingdom of God. And her missionary call required her to remain nonpolitical and submissive to
the government. But as Arlene waited to see if this new government would allow her school to reopen that fall, she needed all the
encouragement she could get.

*November 7, 1975, Friday*

*Rejoice always. Anyone can rejoice when the pathway of life is smooth! Anyone can give thanks in a time of victory. Most people pray in times of real trouble. But I ask you, My Disciple, to pray constantly—without ceasing—in My Spirit. Do not quench My Spirit with your doubts and self-pity, but rejoice in all circumstances, even those that to you seem to be evil, for I can bring good out of them. Abstain from evil yourself as you test the spirits. Heed My prophecies for they are given to warn you, to exhort you, and to comfort you. My Will is for you to give thanks at all times.*

 ## Questions for Reflection/Discussion

1. How did Arlene respond to the political tensions of 1975 Ethiopia?

2. Is there any political tension between you and a friend? What are you hoping for in that situation?

3. "Rejoice always," says the apostle. What are you rejoicing about right this minute?

# ✚ *Message 38*

Now at the festival he used to release a prisoner for them, anyone for whom they asked. Now a man called Barabbas was in prison with the insurrectionists who had committed murder during the insurrection. So the crowd came and began to ask Pilate to do for them according to his custom. Then he answered them, "Do you want me to release for you the King of the Jews?" For he realized that it was out of jealousy that the chief priests had handed him over. But the chief priests stirred up the crowd to have him release Barabbas for them instead. Pilate spoke to them again, "Then what do you wish me to do with the man you call the King of the Jews?" They shouted back, "Crucify him!" Pilate asked them, "Why, what evil has he done?" But they shouted all the more, "Crucify him!"

Mark 15:6–14 (NRSVue)

The revolution was openly anti-American. Arlene, therefore, fell under suspicion. She could hardly blend into the crowd since she was often the only white face. An Ethiopian friend reported that someone from the Ministry of Information was asking questions about her.

Arlene radioed the Ministry of Public Health to press them about the opening of her school. They said there would be a meeting on Monday, but for now, there was no definite word. Later that day, she received this message from the Lord.

*November 8, 1975, Saturday*

*There are those who are jealous of you as some were jealous of Me in My earthly ministry. Satan loves to use jealousy to attack My servants. You must hold on to Me in faith and I will be faithful to you. I will protect you. I will keep you from harm and give you My Love and strength to comfort you when others condemn you falsely. Be not afraid of what others may say or do. You are responsible to Me. Seek only My direction. In Love, be steadfast—no matter what others may say.*

# ✠ Questions for Reflection/Discussion

1. How do you think Jesus' friends felt when they heard the crowds shouting, "Crucify him!"?

2. How would Arlene's experience of being a minority in Mettu, Ethiopia, have been different from being a minority in her hometown of Sioux Center, Iowa?

3. Have you ever said to someone, "I will protect you"?

## ✛ *Message 39*

In the year that King Uzzi'ah died I saw the Lord sitting upon a throne, high and lifted up; and his train filled the temple. Above him stood the seraphim; each had six wings: with two he covered his face, and with two he covered his feet, and with two he flew. And one called to another and said:

> "Holy, holy, holy is the LORD of hosts;
> the whole earth is full of his glory."

And the foundations of the thresholds shook at the voice of him who called, and the house was filled with smoke. And I said: "Woe is me! For I am lost; for I am a man of unclean lips, and I dwell in the midst of a people of unclean lips; for my eyes have seen the King, the LORD of hosts!"

Then flew one of the seraphim to me, having in his hand a burning coal which he had taken with tongs from the altar. And he touched my mouth, and said: "Behold, this has touched your lips; your guilt is taken away, and your sin forgiven." And I heard the voice of the Lord saying, "Whom shall I send, and who will go for us?" Then I said, "Here am I! Send me."

Isaiah 6:1–8 (RSV)

The next day when Arlene was at worship, there was an altercation outside the church building. The police and an official from the Ministry of Information were there to close the service and send everyone away, falsely claiming that the worship service was a political meeting. A miracle of nature occurred—reminiscent of biblical stories like the plagues, Joshua's hornets, Balaam's talking donkey, and the disciples catching the 153 fish. On that Sunday in Mettu, bees suddenly swarmed out of a hive and chased the police away. The complete story is told in the book *Iowa Ethiopia*. The worship inside was so absorbing that Arlene was unaware of the events outside until after the service.

The Sunday bees were followed on Tuesday by a radio call from the ministry that schools were to open the following Monday.

Arlene immediately began sending letters, telegrams, and runners out to her students: *Come to school!*

November 13, 1975, Thursday

> *The sacrifice of thanksgiving gladdens My heart. When you come into My Presence, let it be in a spirit of praise. When you make your fresh vows of commitment to Me each morning, let it be in a spirit of praise and thanksgiving—not in heaviness as if it were a burdensome duty to offer your life afresh to Me. Let it be in the spirit of My Servant Isaiah: "Here am I. Send me." Let Me touch your lips afresh each morning with a burning coal. Let Me anoint you each day with My Spirit of gladness.*

## ✚ Questions for Reflection/Discussion

1. Which biblical persons besides Isaiah saw angels?

2. When have you experienced a miracle involving the natural world?

3. When was a time you said to the Lord, "Here am I, send me"?

# 1976
## January 27 to December 18

Jan 27, 1976 · Tuesday ·

Isaiah 53:3-5 "He was wounded for our transgressions, he was bruised for our iniquities; upon Him was the chastisement that made us whole, and with His stripes we are healed."

Prophecy: "In your present suffering, My child, you have not yet been bruised as I was for your sakes. I was wounded for your disobedience and took punishment so that you might not have to bear the brunt of your sins. I was despised by the authorities and forsaken even by My friends when man's jealousy condemned Me to die for you and all mankind. Will you not gladly live for Me?"

So busy again today and linens and equipment in the hospital almost nil for Pediatrics nrsg care. Hard to supervise 9 students — then teach five hours besides. Called for O.B. case c̄ cord prolapse but told them again that I could not do O.B. work while I have the whole school to myself. Sought the Lord to lift my discouragement and self pity. Feel the enemy's attacks on me and can't break through this. Irritable and complaining --- refrigerator still not working. Have

# ✛ *Message 40*

We despised him and rejected him—a man of sorrows, acquainted with bitterest grief. We turned our backs on him and looked the other way when he went by. He was despised, and we didn't care.

Yet it was our grief he bore, our sorrows that weighed him down. And we thought his troubles were a punishment from God, for his own sins! But he was wounded and bruised for our sins. He was beaten that we might have peace; he was lashed—and we were healed!

Isaiah 53:3–5 (TLB)

Two and a half months passed by without Arlene recording a message from the Lord in her journal. During this interlude, she was attending to her new students, continuing to work as a midwife in the O.B. ward, celebrating the American Christmas (December 25) and her fifty-second birthday (January 3) along with the Ethiopian Christmas (January 7), and struggling with her cough (wondering if it was pneumonia but not having a way to be certain).

Also during this time, Arlene's spiritual commitment continued to deepen. The *sidet* (persecution) at her church strengthened the passion of the worshipers. The services were electric, and she joined with fellow believers for prayer several nights a week. This Ethiopian band of Pentecostal Christians was becoming more and more like those early Christians in the book of Acts.

Among Arlene's greatest influences during this season of life were the Evangelical Sisterhood of Mary and their leader Mother Basilea Schlink. In December, Arlene traveled to Addis Ababa for Ministry of Public Health meetings. Her trip coincided with a visit to Ethiopia by two of the Sisters of Mary, who were staying in the same guest house. She was able to meet with them on eight occasions and even attend a retreat they led. These meetings along with Mother Basilea's books had an impact on Arlene for years to come.

At the dawn of each new year, Arlene always dedicated the first few pages of her journal to writing a summary of the year gone by.

In this year's summary, she examined multiple facets of her personal, professional, social, church, family, and spiritual life. Arlene wrote, *I must not only accept my cross but value it*, along with this quote from Mother Basilea:

> *Your cross may oppress you today, but it will transfigure you tomorrow and lift you up to heaven. Value it highly.*

On that first day of 1976, Arlene remembered in her journal how Jesus was disgraced and tortured. That month, the theme of suffering—Christ's suffering as well as each Christian's—wove throughout her journal entries, culminating in the following message.

*January 27, 1976, Tuesday*

> *In your present suffering, My child, you have not yet been bruised as I was for your sake. I was wounded for your disobedience and took punishment so that you might not have to bear the brunt of your sins. I was despised by the authorities and <u>forsaken</u> even by My friends when jealousy condemned Me to die for you and all people. Will you not gladly live for Me?*

## Questions for Reflection/Discussion

1. Were you ever punished for someone else's wrongdoing?

2. Think back to a time you were a new student somewhere. What's a memory from your first days of school?

3. What author of your lifetime has had the kind of impact on you that Mother Basilea had on Arlene?

 *Message 41*

So we can say with confidence,

> "The Lord is my helper;
> I will not be afraid.
> What can anyone do to me?"

Remember your leaders, those who spoke the word of God to you; consider the outcome of their way of life, and imitate their faith. Jesus Christ is the same yesterday and today and forever.

Hebrews 13:6–8 (NRSVue)

When a medical colleague of Arlene's got married, the hospital staff were all talking about the wedding. Arlene, however, hadn't attended because she hadn't been invited. She consoled herself with knowing that she wouldn't have felt comfortable with all the dancing and drinking that would have been going on—but she still felt left out. She wrote in her journal,

> *ALL the other doctors and nurses (even the Russians) went. It was undoubtedly his way of "persecuting" Christians—but on the basis of being hospital staff let alone Dresser School staff for 4 years—I should have been invited.*

Her newly married colleague was angry with the church and had told her, "The church is not helping the revolution—*Ethiopia Tikdem* [Ethiopia First]—but is against the culture and has followed imperialists." Arlene wanted to point out that he and his future wife would be wearing imperialist-style wedding clothes, would be served from imperialist-style tables and dishes, and would ride to the wedding in cars, not on mules. But she held her tongue.

The lack of a wedding invitation, however, was only a small part of a much larger and more serious issue. Three church buildings in the area had been burned down, most likely by revolutionaries.

*February 4, 1976, Wednesday*

> *Do you believe that I am the same—in all your yesterdays?*
> *I have loved you when you were rejected by others,*
> *protected you when you were endangered by others,*
> *guided you when you were confused by others.*
> *My Love for you is constant, unchanging, unconditional.*
> *I am with you NOW in this disheartening situation!*
> *Claim my power to rule in it—to overrule the enemy who is*
> *trying to distract your gaze from Me.*
> *I SHALL BE WITH YOU IN ALL YOUR TOMORROWS.*
> *Trust in Me now!!!*

## ✚ Questions for Reflection/Discussion

1. "Remember your leaders . . . and imitate their faith," says the writer of the book of Hebrews. Whose faith is a model to you?

2. Have there been times when you were angry with the church? Why?

3. When have you been excluded because of your Christian faith?

# ✚ *Message 42*

I will instruct thee and teach thee in the way which thou shalt go:
I will guide thee with mine eye.

Psalm 32:8 (KJV)

The first weekend of February, Arlene was still coughing. She prayed for strength amid weakness as she wrote the exams for the following Monday. Friday evening found her at a prayer meeting. When her friend Mersha asked for prayer for his cold, Arlene noted that she was glad to pray for others but hesitated to ask for prayer for herself.

On Saturday, she went shopping for vegetables. Although there had been no fresh vegetables to buy for six weeks, today she was able to find tomatoes, lettuce, carrots, and celery. But she still couldn't find fuel for her kerosene refrigerator and knew she would run out soon.

At church that night, a prophet said to the congregation, "Let your hearts be humbled."

The next morning, Arlene woke from an eerily vivid dream. She dreamed that she had suddenly been required to leave Mettu, to turn in her house key and go. After writing about the dream in her journal, she recorded that God's presence was especially real to her that morning, including this message.

*February 8, 1976, Sunday*

*My child, you have been set on a pedestal at times by members of your family, prayer group, or <u>church</u>! Do not let people put God-images on you. Your calling is to help them find a vision of Me—to exalt Me as Master, so that I can truly bless them and guide their lives. You cannot "play God," for your feet are of clay. When they try to exalt you, turn them to Me as the Source. As you humble yourself, I will be exalted in you. The greatest shall become the least. The humble shall be used mightily in My Kingdom.*

## ☩ Questions for Reflection/Discussion

1. Are you someone, like Arlene, who hesitates to ask for prayer for yourself? Have you recently asked someone to pray for you?

2. In what way does the sentence "Let your heart be humbled" resonate with you today?

3. Have you experienced a dream that you understood to be a message from the Lord?

# ✚ *Message 43*

> If you take away from the midst of you the yoke,
>> the pointing of the finger, and speaking wickedness,
> if you pour yourself out for the hungry
>> and satisfy the desire of the afflicted,
> then shall your light rise in the darkness
>> and your gloom be as the noonday.
> And the LORD will guide you continually,
>> and satisfy your desire with good things,
>> and make your bones strong;
> and you shall be like a watered garden,
>> like a spring of water,
>> whose waters fail not.
>
> Isaiah 58:9b–11 (RSV)

The yoke, the pointing of the finger, and the gloom that Isaiah referenced became realities for Arlene. When violence erupted from both sides of the political divide, the government instituted nightly curfews beginning at 10:00 p.m. If a church meeting went long, everyone bunked in overnight. The leaders of the Gore and Mettu churches held meetings to plan their responses to expected persecutions.

By mid-February, Arlene had poured the last bit of kerosene into her refrigerator's reservoir. She wondered if the hospital's supply truck would arrive in time to keep her fridge in operation. The following whisper from the Lord paraphrased Scripture, reaffirming her mission to care for the people of Ethiopia but also asserting that she had a role to play amid all the angry voices that swirled around her.

*February 25, 1976, Wednesday*

> *You are to pour yourself out for the weak and hungry, the sick and distressed. You are to stop those who would speak evil or critical or slandering words. In obedience, follow My commissioning. Then I shall guide you continuously and*

*give you health and light even in the dark moments of your life. You shall be unfailing like a spring and peaceful like a watered garden.*

 *Questions for Reflection/Discussion*

1. Message 43 says, "You are to stop those who would speak evil or critical or slandering words." How might this relate to your own social media participation?

2. Isaiah says, "Then shall your light rise in the darkness and your gloom be as the noonday." When has there been gloom in your life?

3. How are you experiencing God's provision for you today?

# ✚ *Message 44*

> But the Lord stood by me and gave me strength to proclaim the message fully, that all the Gentiles might hear it. So I was rescued from the lion's mouth. The Lord will rescue me from every evil and save me for his heavenly kingdom. To him be the glory for ever and ever. Amen.
>
> 2 Timothy 4:17–18 (RSV)

Mister Channyalow came to the O.B. ward to deliver a transcribed radio message from the head administrator of the Ministry of Public Health (MPH): Arlene Schuiteman was ordered to appear at the MPH in Addis Ababa right away. No reason was given.

Two days later, Arlene flew to Addis, and the following day she was at the MPH office. She was told that she was to move immediately to the city and work at St. Paul's Hospital as a clinical nursing instructor. This was nonnegotiable. After she returned to the mission guesthouse, she had a restless night of weeping over her impending departure from her beloved Mettu.

March 2 was Battle of Adowa Day, a national holiday, which meant that all of the offices were closed. Arlene learned of a prayer meeting being held at Bethel Church, so she joined a large crowd gathered there. Later that night, Arlene copied Isaiah 41:9b–13 (RSV) into her journal, noting,

> *God ministered to me and spoke especially through Isaiah 41.*

This Scripture was today's whisper to Arlene from the Lord.

*March 2, 1976, Tuesday*

> *You are my servant, I have chosen you and not cast you off.*
> *Fear not for I am with you. Be not dismayed for I am your God.*
> *I will strengthen you, I will help you. I will uphold you with*
> *my <u>victorious</u> <u>right</u> <u>hand</u>. Behold all who are incensed against*
> *you shall be put to shame <u>and</u> confounded. Those who strive*
> *against you shall be as nothing and shall perish. You shall seek*

*those who contend with you but you shall not find them. Those
who war against you shall be as nothing at all. For I the Lord
your God hold your right hand. It is I who say to you, Fear not.
I will help you.*

## ✚ Questions for Reflection/Discussion

1. Have you observed anyone recently who was asked to speak in the presence of antagonistic forces? Where did that person's strength seem to come from?

2. Was there a time in your life when you were required to relocate against your wishes?

3. What is there in Message 44 (from Isaiah 41) that is especially meaningful to you today?

# ✚ *Message 45*

"I am the vine, you are the branches. Those who abide in me and I in them bear much fruit, because apart from me you can do nothing. Whoever does not abide in me is thrown away like a branch and withers; such branches are gathered, thrown into the fire, and burned. If you abide in me and my words abide in you, ask for whatever you wish, and it will be done for you. My Father is glorified by this, that you bear much fruit and become my disciples."

John 15:5–8 (NRSVue)

After having lived in Mettu for nine and a half years, Arlene was given one week to move to Addis Ababa. She returned to Mettu to pack up her life. Members of her church prayed that the government would change its mind. But they had to pray quietly because spies were lurking to report anyone caught speaking against the government. Arlene arrived at the Ministry of Public Health in Addis Ababa on the afternoon of her deadline and was handed the roster of students she would be teaching the following Monday.

While teaching at the capital city hospital, she was no longer on O.B. call, and she had her weekends free. The students assigned to Arlene had already failed their national exam, and it was her task to see if their education could be reclaimed. After two months under Arlene's tutelage, four of the students were certified, and three were set back again. But the MPH had more plans for Arlene. She was assigned to a committee to revise the curriculum of the School of Nursing. She also was asked to present lectures to the second-year nursing students and scheduled to nursing duties in the wards. But she would soon be required to move out of the mission guesthouse. And her mail was not being forwarded properly. Telephone service throughout the city was erratic. Her ongoing mission seemed less certain all the time. She began to experience self-pity (which she considered an idol to her own ego) and discouragement (which she considered disbelief). She wrote the following prayer of confession in her journal:

*I condemn this sin of self-pity. Jesus, I need your judgement and chastening. I will not let you go until you change my self-pity into compassion for others.*
*There is only one way—the way of the cross—and Satan is trying to deter us from reaching the Kingdom of eternal joy.*
*I must surrender to suffering.*
*I must bless those who persecute and revile me.*
*I must be "refuse," a door-mat when called to suffer unjustly.*
*I must bear patiently—hardships, <u>loneliness</u>, family troubles.*
*I MUST recognize the reason why I avoid the cross, avoid suffering, chastening, and embarrassment: PRIDE!*
*I MUST look at the Father whose heart is full of love for me!*
*He chose the cross best fitted for me and hides a treasure in it.*
*My Lord, Jesus, You are the crucified Lord and the Crossbearer. I have chosen You as my Lord, given You my will and my love, desiring to follow You. Hear my plea: may you never have to say of me, "You are not worthy of Me; you cannot be My disciple," because I do not want to carry my cross. Grant me the grace to say, "Yes Father" to every cross, trusting that it has been prepared for me personally and comes from the loving hands of the Father. It will bring me an abundance of divine blessing. Grant me to rejoice in my sufferings because they transform me for Your Kingdom of joy and glory—and also give me intimate fellowship with You, my Lord Jesus, here on earth, and let me taste eternal joy.*

The day Arlene wrote the above confession, she attended an evening prayer meeting and responded to an invitation to stand in renewal of her desire to be a disciple of Jesus. A day later, the whispers from the Lord resumed.

*May 25, 1976, Tuesday*

*You are now entering into a new phase of ministry in which there will be more of Me and less of you. The things you need will be drawn to you effortlessly, and My work will be done through you without strain. Abide in Me—and let My creativity flow through you to meet the needs of others whom I will send to you. You need have no fear: the sap will flow through the branch to bear much better fruit as you become more vine-conscious.*

## ✚ Questions for Reflection/Discussion

1. Have you known a student on probation? What was that experience like for them?

2. When have you, like Arlene, responded to an altar call or invitation at a worship service?

3. In what way is Arlene's prayer of confession inspiring to you?

# ✚ *Message 46*

Trust in the LORD with all your heart,
    and do not rely on your own insight.
In all your ways acknowledge him,
    and he will make straight your paths.

Proverbs 3:5–6 (RSV)

Arlene knew very well what her cross was, as she wrote in her journal:

*My Cross = the single life.*

Four of her sisters had not been assigned this life. One sister, Grada, had accepted the single life so that she could care for Ma and support Arlene's missionary service. Arlene had accepted the single life as part of her missionary calling, but now she was questioning this cross. She wasn't questioning the necessity of suffering in the Christian life, but the violence of the Ethiopian revolution alongside the many changes in her own life that brought her to write in her journal,

*At times like this I <u>need</u> a husband and family to give support.*

But she then corrected herself:

*How can I doubt Jesus and His perfect plan for me when He performed so many miracles for me in moving from Mettu???*

The next message she received spoke quite specifically of "one area of your life." Although the message didn't name the area, Arlene surely knew what it was.

*May 26, 1976, Wednesday*

> *You have given much of yourself to Me but you have not given
> all. You are still holding back one area of your life for yourself.
> You trust Me in all other areas, but in this one you are not
> willing to accept My Will. My ways are higher than your ways.
> My Grace is sufficient for you. Release this area to Me. Trust in
> Me to make your paths straight, to make you more effective in
> My service today.*

Although Arlene was committed to carrying her assigned cross, this
didn't mean she had to like it. Cross-bearing was not easy for Jesus,
and it wouldn't be easy for her. But before she could recommit, her
identification of the single life as her particular cross was about to
be seriously called into question.

An evangelist Arlene had known in Mettu visited her in Addis
and introduced her to an evangelist friend of his. Arlene was always
glad to meet another member of the Christian family, especially
one committed to the difficult calling of the itinerant evangelist.
She saw the evangelist's calling as similar to her own missionary
commitment. Little did Arlene understand that she was the tar-
get of an Ethiopian matchmaking ritual. Arlene would record over
thirty additional whispers from the Lord while she was in Ethiopia,
all of them received during a struggle with the government over her
right to be in the country and under the shadow of a tumultuous
courtship with a man named Legesse.

## ✚ Questions for Reflection/Discussion

1. Arlene felt called to bear the difficulties of the single life.
   What difficulty in your life might you call a cross you're
   called to bear?

2. Who other than a family member has been an especially
   supportive partner in your life's work?

3. Is there an area of your life that you are holding back for
   yourself?

 *Message 47*

And the Lord replied, "I myself will go with you and give you success."

For Moses had said, "If you aren't going with us, don't let us move a step from this place. If you don't go with us, who will ever know that I and my people have found favor with you, and that we are different from any other people upon the face of the earth?"

And the Lord had replied to Moses, "Yes, I will do what you have asked, for you have certainly found favor with me, and you are my friend."

Exodus 33:14–17 (TLB)

After multiple visits to the housing office and three months of inching up the waiting list, Arlene's residence in the capital city was finally approved. She had been living alone in Mettu, but since the government seldom approved single occupancies in the city, the mission suggested that Frauke, a young German woman from Hope Enterprises Compound, might become Arlene's roommate. Frauke knew Amharic well and had cared for the poor women of Addis for the past four years. Arlene immediately liked her. Arlene reported in her journal that she was not as tired today:

*Although not radiantly happy, I do feel more like praising.*

*May 27, 1976, Thursday*

*When the pressures of the day seem too great, look quickly to Me. This upward look opens the door in your being for My strength, My wisdom to flow into you and through you into the situations around you. My Grace, my spiritual Power, my Love are sufficient for you! Rest for a moment in Me—then return to your duties with My inner peace in control. When you are the weakest, I can be strongest in you if you surrender to Me full control of each problem.*

## Questions for Reflection/Discussion

1. When are times in your past that you might describe as "radiantly happy"?

2. What are you praising God for right now?

3. What is a song that helps you in your own "upward look"?

# Message 48

But I say, walk by the Spirit.

Galatians 5:16a (RSV)

Years before, back in the United States when Arlene was visiting a member of a supporting church, she overheard one of their children say, "She doesn't look like a missionary."

Arlene indeed looked like a typical American woman. She did not look like an austere person, and she could never be identified by her outward appearance as "religious." She did not wear any uniform except when she was in her official capacity as a medical professional. Neither did she wear the scowl of a judgmental person. She was known for her joy.

She had always taken care with her appearance. After all, she grew up in a "cleanliness is next to godliness" culture, and that perspective followed her onto the mission field. While she avoided attracting attention or anything that she considered prideful, she required her students to wear proper uniforms, and she modeled attentiveness to every aspect of her environment. As a medical professional, she considered attention to detail to be a matter of good health. So it was that on this day—in the midst of teaching, visiting friends in the hospital, sitting in committee meetings, and packing to move—she went to get her hair done.

But one could not know Arlene by her hair or clothes. She heard a distant melody, walked to the beat of a different drummer, and pursued a schedule unknown to almost everyone except the Lord. Messages like the one she recorded today were not intended to convict but, rather, to protect her—to confirm that which she already knew and practiced.

*May 28, 1976, Friday*

*The moments you spend with Me are not wasted. I can compensate for them in your time schedule. You think you are too busy for the upward look. That is Satan's voice, not Mine. I call you to walk with Me through each day: walk by the Spirit! Let Me plan your time schedule and let Me stretch minutes as you give the day to Me. Let it be My day in you. I can open closed doors more easily than you can imagine possible.*

## ✚ Questions for Reflection/Discussion

1. Do you know anyone who, for their own reasons, displays their religion in their clothing?

2. What's the idea behind the expression "Cleanliness is next to godliness"?

3. Is there something especially encouraging to you in Message 48?

 *Message 49*

Now you are the body of Christ and individually members of it. And God has appointed in the church first apostles, second prophets, third teachers, then workers of miracles, then healers, helpers, administrators, speakers in various kinds of tongues. Are all apostles? Are all prophets? Are all teachers? Do all work miracles? Do all possess gifts of healing? Do all speak with tongues? Do all interpret? But earnestly desire the higher gifts.

1 Corinthians 12:27–31 (RSV)

Arlene visited the Sodisk Kilo Housing Place to learn that even though she had approval to rent a house, she was missing the official letter asserting her right to move in. She was informed that she must first make an advance payment of utilities. Once she had proof of payment, she could request the official letter, but then she would have to wait for the wheels of bureaucracy to produce the letter. The right hand of the revolutionary government of Ethiopia didn't always seem to know what the left hand was doing.

Arlene received word that her driver's license had been renewed for two years. That would be useful if she received a new contract and work permit, but she worried that her work permit might expire long before her driver's license.

*May 29, 1976, Saturday*

*I need a Body. My Church is that Body. You—are a part of My Body. My Love will bring healing to the Body and through the Body to the world about you if you are willing to let Me use you as I choose. Each member is important. There is no age limit—only willingness to be used by Me whenever, wherever I call you.*

## Questions for Reflection/Discussion

1. What are some of your key roles in the body of Christ?

2. When has the machinery of bureaucracy been frustrating to you?

3. Message 49 says that "there is no age limit" to usefulness to the Lord. What young person do you know whose faith has inspired you? Who is an elderly person in your circle of friends whose faith inspires you?

 *Message 50*

Be careful—watch out for attacks from Satan, your great enemy. He prowls around like a hungry, roaring lion, looking for some victim to tear apart. Stand firm when he attacks. Trust the Lord; and remember that other Christians all around the world are going through these sufferings too.

After you have suffered a little while, our God, who is full of kindness through Christ, will give you his eternal glory. He personally will come and pick you up, and set you firmly in place, and make you stronger than ever. To him be all power over all things, forever and ever. Amen.

1 Peter 5:8–11 (TLB)

Arlene reported to her supervisor that two of her remedial students were now ready for certification. One student, however, was not passable and should be removed from the program. At that meeting, Arlene learned that the government was looking for an Ethiopian who could replace her. She, too, it seemed, might be removed.

Arlene spent the afternoon praying and journaling. What was God's plan? Could she hope to return to work in Mettu? Did God intend this city contract to end her time in Ethiopia? Did he want her to move to the rental house if she would merely be leaving the city soon? Reflecting on all this, she wrote,

*I feel like a plant with the roots exposed.*

*June 1, 1976, Tuesday*

*Satan is the great deceiver. When he cannot claim your heart by luring you into his temptations, he will try to make you believe that you are too weak or too tired—and especially that you are too busy. Stand firm on My promises. In your weakness My strength will be perfected. In your weakness of spirit and mind and body, rest in Me and be refilled and renewed and refreshed. Let Me take dominion.*

### ✚ Questions for Reflection/Discussion

1. What should you watch for to discern whether you are under attack from your enemy, the "roaring lion"?

2. Are you acquainted with a Christian in another part of the world who is undergoing a struggle today?

3. What was one of God's promises to Arlene?

 *Message 51*

"Come to me, all who labor and are heavy laden, and I will give you rest. Take my yoke upon you, and learn from me; for I am gentle and lowly in heart, and you will find rest for your souls. For my yoke is easy, and my burden is light."

Matthew 11:28–30 (RSV)

Arlene received word that a new work contract for her was being prepared and would be ready for signing in a few days. Although it would be good for only three months, until October 11, it was better than nothing. A colleague at the hospital told her that it wouldn't be renewed after October, but Arlene took a chance anyway and moved into the rental house.

Legesse, the Ethiopian evangelist she had met a few weeks earlier, stopped by the new house to say hello and see if he could help with any unpacking chores. As he left, he said to Arlene, "Let me know when you receive a vision."

What vision? Arlene wondered. And since they were not especially close friends, why would he say such a thing to her? Did he know something she didn't know? Did he have the gift of knowledge? Or prophecy?

By the end of that day of unpacking, she hadn't received a vision, but she did receive the following message.

*June 7, 1976, Monday*

> *Come unto Me and I will refresh you. When you are weary, heavy laden with anxiety, troubled in your heart, you do not need to depend on others. You can look to Me and lift the loads to Me. Release them into My hands in the prayer of surrender and pray in the Spirit. Return to your work refreshed by My Spirit. When you are yoked to Me, your burdens will become lighter. Learn from Me the secret of surrender.*

## Questions for Reflection/Discussion

1. Jesus was known as a rabbi, a teacher. In what ways is he your teacher? What's something you've learned from him?

2. Do you know anyone who has had a vision?

3. What are you currently troubled in your heart about? Have you spoken "the prayer of surrender" about it?

 *Message 52*

Since then we have a great high priest who has passed through the heavens, Jesus, the Son of God, let us hold fast our confession. For we have not a high priest who is unable to sympathize with our weaknesses, but one who in every respect has been tempted as we are, yet without sin. Let us then with confidence draw near to the throne of grace, that we may receive mercy and find grace to help in time of need.

Hebrews 4:14–16 (RSV)

Arlene took off a couple of days from the hospital so she could create a home in the rental house. She hired a man for $3 a day to repaint the rooms. He was neat and steady at his task, and Arlene couldn't be more pleased.

To thank Arlene for doing this, Frauke brought her an African violet with a note drawn from Psalm 9:

I will give thanks to the LORD with all my heart.
I will be glad and exult in Thee,
for you have maintained my cause.

Arlene wrote in her journal,

*Dear God, how I praise you for lifting my burdens.*

*June 8, 1976, Tuesday*

*When you are weak remember that I am your High Priest interceding for you. Satan's nagging voice will make you condemn yourself and lose heart. In My Love, there is not condemnation but forgiveness of sin. My Holy Spirit convicts you to repent and accept My Power to overcome sin in your life—to receive mercy and help in each need. Hold fast to your confession of faith in Me and let My forgiveness bring joy.*

## Questions for Reflection/Discussion

1. Who is a worker you remember who was "neat and steady," delighting you with the result?

2. What little thing has brought you joy recently, like Frauke's African violet?

3. "Let My forgiveness bring joy." For what do you need to ask forgiveness right now?

# Message 53

For God did not give us a spirit of timidity but a spirit of power and love and self-control.

2 Timothy 1:7 (RSV)

Although Arlene was physically tired from the days of moving house, she was happy. She loved the sense of forward momentum, of accomplishing something.

On this day, she spent the morning back in her uniform at the hospital in committee meetings, working out guidelines for future instructors. She went home to help Frauke move into the bedroom situated at the back of the house, but then the housing authorities arrived and announced that no more boxes could be unpacked until certain bills were paid in advance.

Arlene wondered if this was simply a miscommunication or an attempted extortion.

After a lengthy discussion, the officers understood that no more fees were forthcoming, and they took their leave.

*June 10, 1976, Thursday*

*Fear robs you, My child, of your inner peace and composure. Fear is of Satan when it paralyzes you or distorts your true vision. The gift of discernment is given you <u>not</u> to make you fear—but to pray. You have received the gift of the Holy Spirit that you may minister to the needs about you with courage and in the power of My Name. My perfect Love casts out fear. You can take authority over Satan's attacks and keep a sound mind. During his attacks, claim My Victory.*

## Questions for Reflection/Discussion

1. When have you experienced the injustice of a governmental official?

2. Arlene loved to sing. Her roommate Frauke knew German, English, and Amharic; Arlene knew Dutch, Nuer, English, and a bit of Amharic. What's a song they might have sung together?

3. How would you fill in this prayer? "Lord, I am afraid of _____. In the power of the name of Jesus, and through Christ's love, I take authority over my enemy. I invite inner peace, clarity of vision, and a sound mind. Help me to be your minister in this situation. Amen."

# ✚ *Message 54*

"I am the bread of life. Your ancestors ate the manna in the wilderness, and they died. This is the bread that comes down from heaven, so that one may eat of it and not die. I am the living bread that came down from heaven. Whoever eats of this bread will live forever, and the bread that I will give for the life of the world is my flesh."

The Jews then disputed among themselves, saying, "How can this man give us his flesh to eat?" So Jesus said to them, "Very truly, I tell you, unless you eat the flesh of the Son of Man and drink his blood, you have no life in you. Those who eat my flesh and drink my blood have eternal life, and I will raise them up on the last day, for my flesh is true food, and my blood is true drink. Those who eat my flesh and drink my blood abide in me and I in them. Just as the living Father sent me and I live because of the Father, so whoever eats me will live because of me. This is the bread that came down from heaven, not like that which the ancestors ate, and they died. But the one who eats this bread will live forever."

John 6:48–58 (NRSVue)

Frauke's friends brought the last load of her possessions to the house on Saturday, the day that Arlene's good friend Marian visited as their first overnight guest. The next day would be quite full for Arlene, beginning with an early departure to take Marian to the airport, followed by morning worship, a wedding, visiting with friends from Mettu, and evening worship.

But she found time in the cracks of the day for private communion with the Lord, including this message:

*June 13, 1976, Sunday*

*My Love is filling you—every fiber of your being. My Love is sufficient for all the needs of those about you.*

When Arlene arrived home that night, all was quiet—until Frauke's friends carried her in and put her to bed. Apparently, she had experienced some kind of nervous breakdown at their church. Before going to sleep, Arlene wrote in her journal,

*She is a dear person. Jesus, you can help both of us.*

## ✚ Questions for Reflection/Discussion

1. What is one of your favorite Communion songs?

2. This day in Arlene's life was astonishing in its range of events. How do you maintain your equilibrium on such days?

3. What is one of your favorite songs about the love of God?

# *Message 55*

The temptations in your life are no different from what others experience. And God is faithful. He will not allow the temptation to be more than you can stand. When you are tempted, he will show you a way out so that you can endure.

1 Corinthians 10:13 (NLT)

Their new house was near the cage where Haile Selassie's lions were housed. The revolutionary government had deposed the emperor but kept his lions, an icon of Ethiopia. Arlene and Frauke now woke each morning at 5:00 to the sound of lions roaring. After her breakdown last Sunday, Frauke had been prescribed medication and bedrest—but these lions weren't doing much to help.

In addition to Frauke's struggle, Arlene was also concerned about one of her remedial students who had threatened to kill himself. One of Arlene's colleagues told her that he feared what her remedial student might do if she failed him in her course. Arlene did indeed wonder if he might turn violent, not only against himself but against his teacher. She prayed,

> *I commit him into your Hands. Please save him and pluck him out of Satan's wicked hands. Deliver him.*

The Ministry of Public Heath lost Arlene's contract, so she had to sign another one before classes could begin. One hundred and twenty-six new students were to arrive that week, and Arlene would be their lecturer in obstetrics.

By Sunday morning, she was running out of steam, so she prayed, *Lord God, today I need you to speak to my heart, to feed and water me spiritually.* She went to church and was delighted to discover how enthusiastic the choir was—they even clapped! How very reserved this city church was compared to her home congregation in Mettu.

*June 20, 1976, Sunday*

*Satan is trying to distract you from My true purpose for your life. The devil knows the best way to attack you—your weakest spot. He can use uncommitted people to wear down your resistance to his wiles. The Father never tempts His children but He allows Satan to exist during this present time. My strength is always available to you: in every temptation I can make a way out, even where to your eyes there is <u>no</u> way! I can use the devil's temptation to test your faith, your surrender. I will bring you through to greater Victory—if you <u>claim</u> the Power of My Blood over the situation.*

## ✚ Questions for Reflection/Discussion

1. What do you suppose was Arlene's "weakest spot"? What's yours?

2. Message 55 says, "I can make a way out, even where to your eyes there is <u>no</u> way!" What situation can you think of in which, to your eyes, there is no way forward?

3. Arlene prayed for God to feed and water her spiritually. Can you imagine praying that same prayer? If so, how might you rephrase it?

## *Message 56*

> But the Holy Spirit produces this kind of fruit in our lives: love, joy, peace, patience, kindness, goodness, faithfulness, gentleness, and self-control. There is no law against these things!
>
> Those who belong to Christ Jesus have nailed the passions and desires of their sinful nature to his cross and crucified them there. Since we are living by the Spirit, let us follow the Spirit's leading in every part of our lives.
>
> Galatians 5:22–25 (NLT)

Arlene's prayer for her spirit to be fed and watered was answered quickly. Early the next morning, June 21, she was awakened suddenly from a deep sleep with a powerful awareness of Christ's presence. In what she referred to as "a special anointing from Jesus," she experienced a rush of assurance of Jesus' love for her—an emotional, spiritual, and even physical sensation. This "anointing" continued throughout that week and then occurred regularly over the next two months. She also received seven messages from the Lord during this extraordinary season.

Things were getting busy at the hospital with the incoming students, more committee work, and exams to prepare. The work was both tiring and invigorating—she was doing what she loved.

*June 26, 1976, Saturday*

> *My beloved child, go forth with your head held high, a smile on your lips and a song in your heart, for I go before you to prepare the way for this new ministry. I am with you <u>and</u> within you. You have nothing to fear. My Love surrounds you like a great shield, protecting you from all evils, doubts, uncertainties and fears. Keep your eyes on Me. I lead the way—today.*
>
> *Your thinking processes are now being directed by My Holy Spirit to calm, clear, positive, creative thinking. It has been*

*a necessary part of your new ministry that you have been
acquainted with evil so that you might learn how to deal with
it. Be patient. Be persevering. Let Me love through you those
who have deep needs. Keep surrendered to Me not to them.*

Michael, the evangelist who had introduced Arlene to Legesse,
invited her out for dinner and conversation. She didn't yet know
that he was paving the way for the next step in the matchmaking
journey. That step occurred two days later when Legesse stopped
by for two hours late in the afternoon, graciously excusing himself
before she could invite him to stay for dinner.

---

## ✚ Questions for Reflection/Discussion

1. Have you ever had an experience similar to what Arlene
   called "a special anointing from Jesus"?

2. In the past, what especially prepared you for your current work in the kingdom of God? How are your present
   circumstances preparing you for your future work?

3. Message 56 contains simple, practical reminders to hold
   your head high, smile, and sing! Although it's hard to
   imagine that Arlene needed these reminders, it seems she
   did. When do you most need these same reminders?

# ✚ *Message 57*

And as the bridegroom rejoices over the bride,
   so shall your God rejoice over you.

                    Isaiah 62:5b (RSV)

   As Arlene's nightly anointings continued, her vitality returned.
Her desire for the "true bridal love of Jesus" was being affirmed
along with her commitment to bear the cross of the single life.

   While Arlene's vitality increased, however, Frauke grew in-
creasingly physically and emotionally exhausted. As long as she
lived and ministered here in the capital city, Frauke couldn't get
the rest she so desperately needed. With Arlene's encouragement,
Frauke arranged to spend a few days at a retreat center forty miles
out in the country on the shores of Lake Bishoftu.

*June 27, 1976, Sunday*

> *Your body is being filled with My love, giving new vitality in
> all things, new harmony. Your heart is being filled with new
> courage, new love radiating through your whole being to draw
> others to Me. My child, you are to reveal Me to others in ways
> beyond your present understanding. Trust Me to release My
> Power in and through you when I bring to you those in need of
> this ministry of My healing Love.*

## ✚ *Questions for Reflection/Discussion*

1. What wedding can you recall in which the bridegroom's
   joy was remarkable?

2. When have you recently experienced a time of refreshment
   to bring healing to your body and spirit?

3. If God were to fill you with new courage today, in what
   ways would you use it?

# ✚ *Message 58*

"Bear fruit that befits repentance."

Matthew 3:8 (RSV)

A great deal happened in a few short weeks. Frauke left for the retreat center where Arlene hoped she would find peace and restoration, and Arlene attended a bicentennial party at the US Embassy where good ole American hot dogs were served.

While Arlene was on her own, Legesse began stopping by the house more regularly as well as calling her on the phone. Sometimes now he said yes when Arlene asked if he'd like to stay for dinner. She enjoyed his company, and since she had many male friends, she didn't think anything of it.

In the meantime, a committee at church was determining whether to curtail church meetings. Their stated reason was to avoid the possibility of persecution, but Arlene suspected another reason and wrote home about it:

> *One woman has been so opposed to the new charismatic movement and has used her influence that all the meetings except the one on Sunday mornings must be stopped! The reason is the FEAR of persecution. We know that persecution has only strengthened churches when it has come. To close down and protect that dead core is like hovering over a corpse. This is what the elders meeting will be concerned about. This paragraph is not for sharing with the public in general but just for you to pray about.*

*July 17, 1976, Saturday*

> *My Spirit is upon you for I have anointed you for this new ministry. My baptism is with the Holy Spirit and with purifying fire. The chaff will be burned, but the wheat will be gathered in to feed many. You have not been chosen for your human heritage but for your spirit of repentance and humility. My gifts can operate best through those who are willing to be cleansed and willing to be used to proclaim My Love.*

## ✚ Questions for Reflection/Discussion

1. When you are away from home for a long time, is there any particular food you miss?

2. Arlene often turned to her mother and sisters for support. To whom do you go?

3. Arlene wrote, "We know that persecution has only strengthened churches when it has come." Do you hold her position, and if so, in what ways is the church strengthened by persecution?

# ✚ *Message 59*

Do not be conformed to this world but be transformed by the renewal of your mind, that you may prove what is the will of God, what is good and acceptable and perfect.

Romans 12:2 (RSV)

Arlene drove out to Lake Bishoftu to visit Frauke. Legesse volunteered to ride along and help with navigation since Arlene hadn't driven out of the capital city in the four months since she arrived. There might be police checkpoints along the way, so Arlene was glad to have another person along.

Frauke welcomed them graciously, but Arlene thought she looked even more exhausted. Then, on the way home, Legesse seemed quiet and preoccupied. When Arlene asked him if anything was wrong, he only smiled and changed the subject.

The following week, Legesse came to the house and stayed until nearly midnight. Arlene began to wonder about the nature of his interest in her. It felt good to have a friend, and it even felt good to have someone think that she was worthy of being liked as more than just a friend. But how should she respond to him without leading him on? Or was the Lord trying to communicate something to her about him? Arlene was a planner who typically pursued methodical, reasonable courses of action. Was the Lord attempting to open her to possibilities she wouldn't otherwise consider? Whatever the Lord was saying, she would be glad to receive it.

*July 23, 1976, Friday*

> *Sometimes I have to allow you to become confused because you are so determined to go ahead of Me in your own strength and will. You are pulled by the world into patterns and pathways I never intended. Let me remake your whole nature, not just the "religious" part of your life. Dedicate to Me your whole life. Let Me transform your whole attitude, your tastes, your preferences. You cannot do this of yourself alone.*

## ⊕ Questions for Reflection/Discussion

1. What are the dangers of being "conformed to this world"?

2. Have you been through a police checkpoint? If so, how did it impact you emotionally?

3. Can you recall a time when you "ran ahead" and it created problems?

# ✚ *Message 60*

O the depth of the riches and wisdom and knowledge of God! How unsearchable are His judgements and how inscrutable His ways!
Romans 11:33 (RSV)

The weather had turned especially dark, rainy, and cold. Arlene had to finish writing a lengthy form letter to her supporting churches, so she didn't write in her journal that week. Legesse also continued to visit, which took more of her time. In her letters home, she didn't mention Legesse specifically. She only said,

*I have many Ethiopian friends visiting me regularly.*

At the end of the week, she returned to her journal and recorded a lengthy conversation in which Legesse had asked many questions about her future plans. He concluded by saying that he had something to ask her but that he would pray more about it first.

Arlene lay awake that night wondering about this question. She finally began to suspect, however, and the following day confessed in her journal that her conversation with Legesse had stolen her peace. The next day was Sunday, and she received the following message.

*August 1, 1976, Sunday*

> *My ways are higher than your ways. When you cannot see the reason, trust in Me to make it clear in My own way and time. I know your <u>deepest</u> needs, not just the superficial. I am changing your circumstances and attitudes as fast as you will let Me. Lift this disappointment, and leave it with Me. When I close a door it is because I will open a better one—when you are ready. Let Me use this frustration. Let Me take the sting out of it. <u>Bask in My Love</u> for you—not the love of others. My love changes not!*

After the message, Arlene wrote in her journal,

*<u>Amen</u>. Hallelujah!*

That afternoon when she returned from church, the young man guarding the gate seemed to have stepped away, which meant that Arlene couldn't get in. So she went out for lunch with a friend and then to the meetings of a spiritual life conference. When she returned that evening, the gate was still locked, and a friend had to climb over the wall to let her into her house.

She soon discovered the reason why the guard was missing: While she had been out that morning, he had robbed all her spare cash, some of her clothes, her wristwatch, and her passport.

When Legesse called that night, she told him what happened and he rushed over to be with her. They didn't speak of his question. After he left, she slept fitfully and had nightmares.

## ✠ Questions for Reflection/Discussion

1. What missionaries did your church support when you were growing up? What impact did that relationship have on you as a child?

2. Have you had a relationship that you hid from your family? If so, why?

3. Have you been the victim of a robbery? If so, what was your journey of healing from the experience?

# ✚ *Message 61*

Blessed is anyone who endures temptation. Such a one has stood the test and will receive the crown of life that the Lord has promised to those who love him. No one, when tempted, should say, "I am being tempted by God," for God cannot be tempted by evil and he himself tempts no one. But one is tempted by one's own desire, being lured and enticed by it; then, when desire has conceived, it engenders sin, and sin, when it is fully grown, gives birth to death.

Do not be deceived, my beloved brothers and sisters.

James 1:12–16 (NRSVue)

After the robbery, Arlene spent every spare moment of the following week filling out police reports, itemizing property, and visiting the embassy to apply for a new passport. In order to submit a police report, however, Arlene soon learned that she needed to commit to a "donation" to the area police fund—not just once, but regular monthly payments.

At the end of the week, she leafed through her journal to find the request she had made two months earlier when she was at her loneliest and lowest. She had written,

*"You have not because you ask not," so I asked.*

She had told God that she needed a husband and a family. She still didn't know if God's intent was to answer her prayer by providing her a husband or by fulfilling her need for family in some other way. What she did know was that her desire for a husband and family indicated the difficulty of the single life—what she called her "Cross." She wrote,

*God what are you trying to show me? About my request or My Cross?*

In her darkest moments, she wondered if God was tempting her. She had a strong suspicion that Legesse wanted to speak to her about marriage. If so, was he an answer to her prayer or a temptation away from her calling?

*August 8, 1976, Sunday*

> *You have said that I tempted you, but this is not true. The devil tempts you to sin. He entices you to listen to sinful thoughts and insinuations which come at you; but you need not give them room in your heart. Whether it is lust or fear or resentment or self-pity, you need not be led into sin if you will resist the first thoughts and claim the power of My Blood over them. The longer you dally with the thoughts, the easier will be Satan's victory. You are a child of God protected by My Shed Blood—if you claim it!*

## ✚ Questions for Reflection/Discussion

1. What is the distinction between "testing" and "tempting"?

2. What is the distinction between "first thoughts" and "sin"?

3. What assurance do you have that God will give you a way out of temptation?

# ✚ *Message 62*

The LORD will keep
your going out and your coming in
from this time forth and for evermore.

Psalm 121:8 (RSV)

Arlene continued to have nightmares, which she assumed was her subconscious trying to cleanse itself in the aftermath of being robbed. Then something truly horrible happened to Frauke at Lake Bishoftu. It was a quiet retreat center and security was minimal. Around midnight on Saturday, August 14, a man in his thirties entered and began rummaging for something to steal. When Frauke heard him, she got out of bed to investigate. When he saw her, he hit her in the head and forced her to the floor. His intent became painfully clear, and Frauke began to pray aloud—not for herself but for the man! She would later tell Arlene that she prayed for him and spoke to him "as if he were my guest. I was not afraid. This was not my doing, but God's." As she spoke, she watched the man's face fade from anger to fear. He suddenly stopped, stood up, and left without hurting her any further or taking anything. Frauke later wrote,

> The blood of Jesus cleanses us from every sin, little or big in human eyes, so there is hope for this poor frightened murderer, too. Arlene, it is good to be alive. I even do not mind my looks (bruises on knees, a few at the body, and just tiny scratches in the face). Satan was active, but Jesus won the victory!

Frauke and her mission decided it was time for her to return to Germany. She told Arlene she would come to Addis Ababa on her way home, but Arlene couldn't wait. There were logistical questions about helping her pack, but she also simply wanted to see her friend. She made plans to go see Frauke at the lake.

In the meantime, Arlene wrote to Grada about the robbery in Addis. She asked her sister not to tell Ma yet. That news could wait until the dust had settled.

Legesse was also waiting. A week and a half went by, and he still hadn't asked his question.

*August 19, 1976, Thursday*

> *Trust in Me to keep you safe by day or by night. You have committed your life to Me. Know that My promises are true. I am faithful and just to keep My Word. Lift up your eyes to Me this morning. Take them off the day's problems and uncertainties. Be certain of My Love; be sure of My Protection. I will keep you from all evil. I will watch over your life!*

## ✚ Questions for Reflection/Discussion

1. What were the ripple effects of Frauke's assault on her as well as her community?

2. Message 62 says, "Trust in Me to keep you safe" and "Be certain of My Love." Arlene could see that Frauke's bruises were real. Did that mean that God didn't wish to keep Frauke safe or that God loved Frauke less than Arlene? And what of Wobitu, who died in childbirth? What of God's love for her and her family?

3. To whom does Frauke's story encourage you to reach out?

# ✚ *Message 63*

Then his mother and his brothers came to him, but they could not reach him for the crowd. And he was told, "Your mother and your brothers are standing outside, desiring to see you." But he said to them, "My mother and my brothers are those who hear the word of God and do it."

Luke 8:19–21 (RSV)

On Saturday, August 21, it was evening when Arlene finally sat down with her journal, writing, *What a day!* Pouring rain had awakened her that morning at 5:00 a.m. Three hours passed before the rain let up a little. Arlene and her friend Rachel caught a break in the storm to drive out of Addis Ababa and bring comfort to Frauke at Bishoftu Lake. They spent the morning listening to Frauke pour out her story of the previous Saturday night when the mercy of God had stared into the face of evil. They prayed together and promised to set aside time for Frauke when she traveled through Addis Ababa the following Monday on her way home to Germany.

Saturdays were now Arlene's weekly fasting day. She expected headaches on fasting days, and today's headache started on her way home from the retreat center. She took a nap that afternoon and then friends stopped by, including Legesse. Even though she was fasting, Arlene made supper for her friends.

When the others finally left, Legesse lingered behind. The time had come for his question. He started by explaining the reason he had seemed troubled that day on their way home from the lake. He had been afraid to tell Arlene the truth. But now God had spoken to his heart, urging him to tell Arlene that he was in love with her. He had come to believe that they should marry. But he knew that this revelation would come as a surprise, so his question was a simple one: Would Arlene join him in praying about the matter? That was an easy request. Yes, she would pray.

When she woke on August 26, she realized that the nightly anointing of Jesus' love had not occurred. It was the same the next morning and the one after that. Then she received this message.

*August 28, 1976, Saturday*

*You were lonely but I have given you a new family. Your new mother and brothers and sisters are those who listen for My Voice and heed My warnings. With them you will find rich fellowship. They may be of many ages, races, denominations, and nationalities—but you will feel that they are your family because they love and obey My Word. You will share My Love with a very large family that extends around the world.*

She suspected she knew how to interpret the message: Her calling to the single life had opened the way to a new family including the sisters from Germany, her fellow missionaries, and her church in Ethiopia—a great family extending far beyond her Iowa upbringing. But she remained open to the possibility of another interpretation: God might ask her to marry a man of a different age, race, and background. There was the possibility that Legesse, a Christian leader and her brother in Christ, had heard the Lord's voice correctly. She would pray. Yes, she would pray.

## ✚ *Questions for Reflection/Discussion*

1. Jesus understood that his biological family was at odds with his ministry family. When have you experienced such a conflict between biological and faith families?

2. When have you experienced someone's understanding of God's will being different from your own?

3. When have you experienced a cultural misunderstanding or cross-cultural conflict?

# ✠ *Message 64*

I've blotted out your sins; they are gone like morning mist at noon!
Oh, return to me, for I have paid the price to set you free.

Isaiah 44:22 (TLB)

When Arlene agreed to pray for anything, there were several things she knew about the process. First, it should begin immediately. There was no need for hesitation, even for a minute. Second, the journey of prayer could take a long time, since it was a journey of discernment through studying the Scriptures and listening to the promptings of the Spirit. Third, it required praying in agreement with other believers. But Arlene needed to be careful about who she asked to pray with her. The possibility of a middle-aged, White, American medical professional marrying a younger, Black, Ethiopian evangelist without schooling or a penny to his name could become a topic for considerable gossip. She wanted the help of prayer warriors but didn't want to create room for unsolicited advice or mockery. She spoke with only a few trusted Ethiopian friends, and they each immediately agreed with her early leanings that marriage to Legesse was not a good idea.

However, Legesse's faith was impressive to Arlene. Having spent six years as a charismatic preacher, he depended on the Lord literally for his daily bread. He had little desire for earthly possessions. He was quiet and kind. She wondered if God wanted to teach her new lessons of trust and obedience through difficult means, including suffering and reproach.

*August 31, 1976, Tuesday*

*When you are tempted, remember that you can call upon Me for strength to overcome. My wisdom will show you the way of victory if you call upon Me. Do not despair because there are many temptations. I, too, was tempted in the wilderness. I will not let the enemy overcome you if you look to Me for help and*

*stand firm in the power of My Victory. Claim My Blood over*
*every temptation. I died for you.*

For the next three months, she would receive no new whisper
from the Lord—and her process of discernment was undergoing
a change. Even though she knew it might be weeks before she received a reply, she wrote to her old friend Vandy for advice. Vandy
(Eleanor Vandevort) was now living stateside, had published a
memoir Arlene loved titled *A Leopard Tamed*, and was one of the
best-humored and wisest persons Arlene knew. She admitted to
Vandy that the idea of marriage was tempting—that it would be
good to finally have a partner to help her at every turn.

## ✚ Questions for Reflection/Discussion

1. Can you think of a poetic image that communicates the
   same idea as "gone like morning mist at noon"?

2. From whom do you seek advice? What small circle of
   people do you trust to speak godly wisdom into your life?

3. Is there anyone with whom you pray on a regular basis?

# ✚ *Message 65*

Do you want more and more of God's kindness and peace? Then learn to know him better and better. For as you know him better, he will give you, through his great power, everything you need for living a truly good life: he even shares his own glory and his own goodness with us! And by that same mighty power he has given us all the other rich and wonderful blessings he promised; for instance, the promise to save us from the lust and rottenness all around us, and to give us his own character.

2 Peter 1:2–4 (TLB)

After his request for her to pray about marriage, Legesse and Arlene had several lengthy conversations. He admitted to her that she was not responding as he had hoped and he was having difficulty sleeping. Together, they agreed to take a break and not see each other for at least two weeks. Within a few days, Legesse called to say that it felt as if a year had gone by. Could he please come over? Arlene agreed and the conversations resumed.

In the wee hours of the morning of Thursday, September 16, the special anointing from the Lord returned—less powerful than before but strong enough to bring her joy and gratitude. She prayed, using the words of Psalm 139: "Search me, O God, and know my heart; test my thoughts. Point out anything you find in me that makes you sad, and lead me along the paths of everlasting life." Longing for sanctification, she wrote in that morning's journal,

*Read 2 Peter 1. It is for me.*

Those verses affirmed that she had been given the tools for a share in God's goodness, a portion of God's own character. These were what she truly wanted.

She was wise enough to know that she couldn't get these blessings on her own. Just as she couldn't summon an anointing, she couldn't create holiness. She could walk the path on which sanctification was most apt to be found, but she knew that sanctification itself would be the Spirit's work. In other words, the way of holiness was not a way of living but rather the road one traveled to meet the Spirit who had the power to change the human heart. And just as the path of healing goes into the doors of a hospital, the path of holiness goes through the doors of the church.

Arlene desperately needed her precious church back in Mettu. Now that she was living in Addis Ababa, she no longer had access to Mettu's vibrant worship, her trusted elders, and their prophecies. That morning she wrote a prayer in her journal:

> *I need Words of Prophecy/Knowledge/Wisdom from God*
> *through some elders. Please, God, speak.*

Arlene then read back through her past couple of years of journals, rejoicing over the written reminders of God's faithfulness she found there. She rediscovered the times that God had whispered directly to her and claimed a message from the previous year by rewriting it in her journal entry for today.

*September 16, 1976, Thursday (first recorded on August 15, 1975)*

> *Have no fear of those in authority over you, but hold them*
> *in respect as My instruments. If you are admonished, pray to*
> *know My Spirit confirming where there is truth. But be subject*
> *in humility to My Spirit that through the word of Wisdom*
> *you may know the truth about yourself. In honesty seek*
> *discernment that you may grow through this correction to be*
> *more usable by Me.*

## ✠ Questions for Reflection/Discussion

1. What practices help you to "learn to know [God] better and better"?

2. What is there about Arlene's faith journey that is especially encouraging to you?

3. What song do you sing to strengthen your faith?

# ✚ *Message 66*

Blessed be the God and Father of our Lord Jesus Christ, who hath blessed us with all spiritual blessings in heavenly places in Christ:

According as he hath chosen us in him before the foundation of the world, that we should be holy and without blame before him in love:

Having predestinated us unto the adoption of children by Jesus Christ to himself, according to the good pleasure of his will, to the praise of the glory of his grace, wherein he hath made us accepted in the beloved.
Ephesians 1:3–6 (KJV)

Arlene finally told her mission supervisor about Legesse's desire to marry her and his certainty that it was God's will. Although Arlene confessed to a posture of willing obedience to whatever the Lord asked of her, she wasn't yet certain that God was asking her to get married—let alone marriage to Legesse. Arlene's supervisor said to her, "When you are uncertain, just continue as you are until you know."

A few days later, Arlene awakened at 4:00 a.m. with waves of Jesus' love pouring over her—twice! She didn't receive a message from the Lord, but she searched again and copied another message from the prior year.

*September 23, 1976, Thursday (first recorded on August 20, 1975)*

*Do not pride yourself on your fine churches for heaven is my throne. The earth is only My footstool. I am not impressed by human titles or accomplishments, but I seek out the one who is humble and contrite in heart who obeys My Word. That is the one whom I use mightily.*

This merciful start provided good footing for a day that would turn tragic, mysterious, and difficult. Arlene arrived at work at 8:00 a.m. to learn that one of her graduate nurses had died at another hospital while receiving anesthesia for a routine procedure.

Then at noon that day, when Arlene stepped outside, she noticed an unusual dark cloud surrounding the sun. The effect, which lasted about an hour, made a double, circular rainbow—a heavenly sign stranger than she had ever seen in life or even in pictures. That afternoon, there was an anti-government rally in the city. The police arrived, shooting live rounds into the crowd, wounding and killing many. Ten of the wounded were brought to Arlene's hospital. She was already busy with the delivery of several babies, including one anencephalic infant who died soon after birth. Coming out of the hospital at the end of her shift, Arlene discovered a flat tire on her car—and once again, she wished she had a partner to help her.

That night around 8:30 p.m., there was an assassination attempt on Mengistu, the revolutionary leader of the Derg government, on Bishafto Road where Legesse had been walking. He heard gunfire and then a bullet whizzed past his head. He dropped to the ground and lay frozen for a long time before warily rising and then running all the way to his apartment. Frightened, he called Arlene—and she was frightened for him. The chaos of the city along with her own conflicted emotions leaned heavily on the decision Arlene knew she must soon make.

## ✚ Questions for Reflection/Discussion

1. What is there in the natural world that especially humbles you?

2. What must it have felt like to care for those who were wounded as the result of police shooting randomly into a crowd?

3. When has someone close to you come through a life-threatening experience?

# ✚ *Message 67*

And when he got into the boat, his disciples followed him. A windstorm suddenly arose on the sea, so great that the boat was being swamped by the waves, but he was asleep. And they went and woke him up, saying, "Lord, save us! We are perishing!" And he said to them, "Why are you afraid, you of little faith?" Then he got up and rebuked the winds and the sea, and there was a dead calm. They were amazed, saying, "What sort of man is this, that even the winds and the sea obey him?"

Matthew 8:23–27 (NRSVue)

Legesse understood Arlene enough to know that there could be no marriage without her family's support, so he urged Arlene to write to them. Instead, her letters spoke of her hope that she would obtain a contract to continue teaching and such things as "How are you getting along with painting the basement?" She never mentioned Legesse. Not yet.

The matter of marriage was seldom far from her mind now. She procured and read Walter Trobisch's book *I Married You*, and she spoke with more and more friends about Legesse's question. They all said it wasn't a good idea. The matchmaker was the only person who seemed to support Legesse's plan.

Then Vandy's response finally arrived.

*You think you will have someone to help you at every turn? Don't kid yourself; chances are you'll end up doing everything for both of you. Somehow or other, it just isn't a bed of roses.*

Vandy's conclusion?

*Marriage has got to be a vocation under God.*

Arlene's head agreed, but her heart grew more uncertain by the day.

Friday, October 8, was the last day of work under her old contract, and she still didn't have a new one. Without a contract, the government could ask her to leave at any moment. It was a perfect storm of uncertainties.

*October 10, 1976, Sunday (first recorded on September 7, 1975)*

> *I have many purposes for the days ahead. Some of them will be dark days. Some will be stormy—but be not afraid. My Peace will abide in you in the midst of storms. You will be lifted over the waves. You will be carried through the darkness in Light that no one can quench. You have nothing to fear. Your faith will be strengthened by my presence. Do not let your fears rock the boat. Be still and know!*

## Questions for Reflection/Discussion

1. After Jesus rebuked the winds and the sea and there was a dead calm, Matthew writes that his disciples were amazed. If you had been on the boat, what would you have thought?

2. What strikes you about Vandy's response to Arlene?

3. What are some of the ways the Lord had been preparing Arlene for the dark days he told her about a year earlier?

## ✠ *Message 68*

The steadfast love of the LORD never ceases,
  his mercies never come to an end;
they are new every morning;
  great is thy faithfulness.

*Lamentations 3:22–23 (RSV)*

Arlene woke up at 3:00 a.m. on Monday morning, but she felt rested. She went outside to see the stars. The moon was bright. The city was quiet. She felt God so near. And in that moment, she sensed release from any responsibility to marry. God had not given her the same call he had given Legesse. The only question now was how to gently disappoint the man.

As for work, she would continue day by day in hopes that a contract would eventually be offered.

*October 11, 1976, Monday (first recorded on September 8, 1975)*

*The new doorway I am opening is not an easy one, but it
will be rewarding. In the Spirit you will be led into deeper
intercessions for those in need. I will teach you much that you
have never learned but it will not be for yourself alone. I know
your innermost thoughts. You need only to pray to be kept in
the center of My highest Will for your life.*

In her rewriting of the prophecy from the prior year, Arlene underlined each word of the final sentence:

*You need only to pray to be kept in the center of My highest
Will for your life.*

## ✚ *Questions for Reflection/Discussion*

1. What formed Arlene's belief in the power of prayer?

2. How did you come to follow Jesus?

3. How will you pass along to the next generation your story of God at work in your life?

# ✚ *Message 69*

I therefore, a prisoner for the Lord, beg you to lead a life worthy of the calling to which you have been called, with all lowliness and meekness, with patience, forbearing one another in love, eager to maintain the unity of the Spirit in the bond of peace.

Ephesians 4:1–3 (RSV)

Although Arlene's supervisor, Sister Dejyetune, didn't have word yet of a new contract, she did have a simple request. She asked Arlene if she would travel to Mettu in early November to administer the national exam to the students at her former dresser school. This request was music to Arlene's ears. Yes, she would go. And again, she copied a message from the prior year.

*October 12, 1976, Tuesday (first recorded on September 9, 1975)*

*I have new plans for your life. Some are beyond your furtherest hopes. In obedient trust they will be fulfilled—but not by striving and straining. Let Me bring these opportunities for service in My timing. Be open. Be receptive. Be loving. Be expectant. Do joyously whatever I give you to do, no matter how small. Be My message to those around you.*

Arlene wouldn't record another message, new or copied, until December. By then, Arlene's Ethiopian journey would be nearing its end.

✚ *Questions for Reflection/Discussion*

1. What's your experience of the worldwide Christian church that lives behind prison bars?

2. Sister Dejyetune must have had great respect for Arlene's integrity to trust sending her back to her former school to proctor the national exam with objectivity. When have you been entrusted with a great responsibility?

3. What has been your own experience with journaling?

# ✚ *Message 70*

Therefore, my beloved, as you have always obeyed, so now, not only as in my presence but much more in my absence, work out your own salvation with fear and trembling; for God is at work in you, both to will and to work for his good pleasure.

Philippians 2:12–13 (RSV)

At the end of October, Arlene gave Legesse her answer. She told him in person but also wrote out her reasons in a letter she handed to him. He could not accept her answer. He had fallen in love, and he really did believe that she was his calling. But he had not tested his discernment within the prayerful community of fellow believers as Arlene ultimately had.

Arlene made her trip to Mettu in November, which was a glorious reunion. When she returned to Addis Ababa, she was told that her contract would not be renewed. Her colleagues and students complained, but their objections did no good. Arlene's mission supervisors planned a visit to the top Ministry of Public Health administrators to see if there was another assignment for her somewhere in the country.

But Arlene's heart was no longer in that fight.

Legesse came to visit. She was at such loose ends that she began to second-guess her decision about marriage. She understood that it would be important to make a clean break and leave the country. Even though her supervisors hadn't yet met with the MPH, she began to pack.

*December 2, 1976, Thursday (first recorded on October 9, 1975)*

*You are My beloved. When you obey My commands, I am abiding within you to work out the details of your life. You need fear nothing but the loss of Me, for I can bring good out of evil and transform this situation. Turn each decision of your life over to Me so that I can fulfill My destiny for your life. I am working out your salvation but you must surrender your will to Me.*

## ✝ *Questions for Reflection/Discussion*

1. How do you reconcile the Bible's uses of the word *fear*, which sometimes castigates it ("Fear not, for I am with you") and other times commends it ("work out your own salvation with fear and trembling")?

2. Have you ever had to give someone a disappointing decision? What did you learn about delivering such a decision?

3. When have you experienced the kind of "glorious reunion" that Arlene had at Mettu?

# ✛ *Message 71*

Each time he said, "No. But I am with you; that is all you need. My power shows up best in weak people." Now I am glad to boast about how weak I am; I am glad to be a living demonstration of Christ's power, instead of showing off my own power and abilities.

2 Corinthians 12:9 (TLB)

Arlene continued to write prayers in her journals on occasion, and on the morning of December 3, she wrote,

*This day—dear Master—is for You to direct. Give me the enthusiasm and wisdom and guidance I need for today. Or if you want me to continue to be "immobilized" and simply waiting, that's okay too. I love You.*

Later in the day, Legesse and the matchmaker came to visit. Legesse insisted that Arlene had already promised to marry him, but she reminded him that he knew this wasn't true. She later confessed to her journal that his tenacity prevented the possibility that her love for him could grow. Even after Arlene's clearly negative responses, he continued to push and press, and a few days later, a new message from the Lord spoke quite specifically into these circumstances.

*December 7, 1976, Tuesday*

*This one who vexes you is a product of the sin of the world. He has set his will deliberately against Mine. You do not need to be afraid of him for I have overcome the world. Keep the protective circle of purifying fire around you so that nothing of evil may enter your spirit to poison you or harm your body. Beware (when you think you are strong) lest you fall through pride or self-righteousness into the enemy's trap—even as this one has strayed into the enemy's clutches. Be wise to protect yourself by claiming My Blood. Let Me stand always between you and him. Leave him to Me. Only My Spirit can save him. Do not resent him or judge him. Judgement is Mine.*

## ✠ Questions for Reflection/Discussion

1. How does Arlene's prayer for this day inspire you?

2. Since the kingdom of heaven has clearly not yet come, what does Jesus mean when he says, "I have overcome the world"?

3. Is there someone in your life right now about whom you need to ask the Lord's help so that you won't be resentful or judgmental?

# ✚ *Message 72*

What a wonderful God we have—he is the Father of our Lord Jesus Christ, the source of every mercy, and the one who so wonderfully comforts and strengthens us in our hardships and trials. And why does he do this? So that when others are troubled, needing our sympathy and encouragement, we can pass on to them this same help and comfort God has given us. You can be sure that the more we undergo sufferings for Christ, the more he will shower us with his comfort and encouragement.

2 Corinthians 1:3–5 (TLB)

At 4:00 p.m. on Tuesday, December 7, Arlene and her mission supervisors visited Mister Fekede at the Ministry of Public Health. His answer was final: Arlene must leave Ethiopia. Arlene journaled,

*I praise the Lord for this is His doing. Now let me arrange all things in peace. Let me follow step by step.*

She wrote to her mother and sister that she was coming home.

Legesse called to say he was trying to arrange a meeting with Arlene's mission supervisor. Her supervisor had departed for Nairobi, but even if a meeting could be arranged, Arlene knew that nothing would come of it.

On Friday, Arlene begin her daily Bible study at 5:00 a.m. Then she recorded a new and specific message from the Lord.

*December 10, 1976, Friday*

*My peace can comfort you in this time of testing and affliction. My merciful peace can wash away your remorse over anything you said or thought or did—or failed to do in this relationship. Give Me all of your nagging thoughts—your true guilts and false accusations from the enemy. As you allow My Spirit to comfort you, I can make you able to comfort others. You will find many who will walk the lonely path you are now* *walking. But you are <u>not</u> <u>alone</u> for I am with you! The blessing of My Presence will enable you to help others to find this same blessing in their times of need.*

## ✚ Questions for Reflection/Discussion

1. According to the apostle Paul, what's one reason for our hardships and trials?

2. What were the differences in each of Arlene's and Legesse's responses to Mister Fekede's decision?

3. When have you felt God's peace in the middle of a confusing or uncertain situation? How did he communicate his peace to you?

# ✚ Message 73

And this is the confidence that we have in him, that, if we ask any thing according to his will, he heareth us. And if we know that he hear us, whatsoever we ask, we know that we have the petitions that we desired of him.

1 John 5:14–15 (KJV)

On the morning of December 16, Arlene was awakened early, immersed in the love of Jesus that felt three times stronger than any anointing she had experienced the previous summer. She wrote in her journal several hymns that came to mind, including this one:

*My Jesus, I love thee, I know thou art mine;*
*For thee, all the follies of sin I resign;*
*My gracious Redeemer, my Savior art thou;*
*If ever I loved thee, my Jesus 'tis now.*

Then she recorded another new prophecy.

*December 16, 1976, Thursday*

*You are to ask for much, My child—but in accordance with my will, for it is higher and better than your will. When you ask in my Name you are asking in accordance with my Nature. You ask for baubles but I want to give you the <u>pearl</u> of great price. You may be confident that I hear your requests and that I am answering the prayers that are made in accordance with My Will. I am more willing to give—than you are to ask for the fullness of My Will to be done in this situation. Ask in trust— in expectancy—so that you may receive.*

## ✚ *Questions for Reflection/Discussion*

1. What is your daily prayer rhythm?

2. What's a song you like to sing to express your love for Jesus? Did you sing it today?

3. Is there something God wants to give you today for which you haven't yet asked?

# ✚ *Message 74*

O Lord, open thou my lips,
    and my mouth shall show forth thy praise.
For thou hast no delight in sacrifice;
    were I to give a burnt offering, thou wouldst not be pleased.
The sacrifice acceptable to God is a broken spirit;
    a broken and contrite heart, O God, thou wilt not despise.
Do good to Zion in thy good pleasure;
    rebuild the walls of Jerusalem,
then wilt thou delight in right sacrifices,
    in burnt offerings and whole burnt offerings;
    then bulls will be offered on thy altar.

Psalm 51:15–19 (RSV)

Arlene was struggling with intestinal trouble which turned out to be a case of ascariasis (roundworm) as a result of her trip to Mettu. Thankfully a prescription of Sulfatrim provided immediate relief. She noted in her journal that it was a small price to pay to be able to visit her old friends, including Pastor Terfa who had been imprisoned as part of the revolutionary government's efforts to bring local leaders under their control.

On Saturday morning, she jotted a letter to Ma and Grada, telling them she still didn't have specific travel plans.

> *I'm eager to see you all but dreading the ice cold weather and re-entry into civilization.*

Her transition out of Africa had begun.

*December 18, 1976, Saturday*

> *My desire is not for sin offerings of bulls or sheep but for a repentant heart. Can you reply with Me to the Father: "I have come to do Thy will." In My earthly Body, I took upon Myself your sins. You have been atoned for by My sacrifice. If you will accept this—My gift of freedom from guilt—you will walk out a*

*new person. Stand on My promises. I will no longer remember the sins that you have offered to me to be nailed to My Cross. Rejoice and be free!*

 *Questions for Reflection/Discussion*

1. What does God want first, before "right sacrifices" that lead to feasting?

2. When did a trip to visit friends cost you physically afterwards?

3. What's a song you sing that refers to the blood of Jesus?

# 1977
## January 13 to December 19

phoned at 10 PM and we talked a long time. He asked for forgiveness.
Wants to see me again before I leave. Says Kebede is back in
town and planned to talk with me. Told me about Merid advising
him to ask forgiveness and leave everything. This was after
my short conversation along the road on Thursday. He wants some
remembrance --- He still feels separated from his friends.

Jan 17 Reading I Peter 4:13 - "Rejoice in so far as you share Christ's
sufferings, that you may also rejoice and be glad when His glory is
revealed".

※ Prophecy - "Suffering has come upon you, My child, but it is only to prove
your faith in Me. Hold fast to My Truth and you shall not be
dismayed when others desert or reproach you for My sake. Remain
steadfast in prayer and I shall overcome this evil assault of the
enemy. Continue to glorify Me in praise and I shall restore
this situation. My Power shall be resting upon you when it is
needed. Go in faith, nothing doubting, when I call you to go in
My Name. Fear not the interference of the enemy. I shall
vindicate My Plan. I shall be glorified in this problem" -
Went to pick up my salary ₱3,052.54 at the CSN
and Commercial Bank. It has been there since Dec 23.
Ato Endasha went c̄ me. Then to Ato Haile Gabriel in MPH

# ✚ Message 75

The Spirit of the Lord GOD is upon me,
     because the LORD has anointed me
to bring good tidings to the afflicted;
     he has sent me to bind up the brokenhearted,
to proclaim liberty to the captives,
     and the opening of the prison to those who are bound;
to proclaim the year of the LORD's favor,
     and the day of vengeance of our God;
     to comfort all who mourn;
to grant to those who mourn in Zion—
     to give them a garland instead of ashes,
the oil of gladness instead of mourning,
     the mantle of praise instead of a faint spirit;
that they may be called oaks of righteousness,
     the planting of the LORD, that he may be glorified.
                                   Isaiah 61:1–4 (RSV)

Christmas came and went with no music in the house. All the records and tapes were either packed up, sold, or given away. Life was sorting, cleaning, burning papers, and trying desperately to catch up with unanswered letters amid drop-in visitors who came to say goodbye or purchase something from the items Arlene needed to sell. There was no such thing as a schedule anymore. Her house was a constant, shuffling mess, and Arlene was grateful Ma couldn't see her now. She prayed, *Please God, prepare the Way through my wilderness today.*

She received the required vaccinations to cross the border home—yellow fever, cholera, and smallpox—and spent a day with side effects, alongside the continuing, aching neuralgia from the medication for her ascariasis.

She hunted through the market for a sweater or two for the trip home, but she struggled to find such items here so close to the equator. Then the police came banging on her door looking for firearms. Why wouldn't they, Arlene wondered, when the gossip around town was that she had been ordered out of the country because she was C.I.A.? Although she knew that story would be funny one day, she wasn't laughing at the moment.

Perhaps worst of all was that her suitor hadn't stopped pursuing her. He came by to say he couldn't stop loving her and couldn't sleep. He couldn't stand the thought that she might hold a grudge against him. But how could he be certain, he wondered, that she didn't hold a grudge against him if he couldn't visit her or call her? Arlene wrote in her journal,

> *We talked. We prayed. We cried. God, what agony. All is darkness.*

She finally told him that her mission supervisor didn't want him to visit her unless the supervisor was present. Arlene knew an Ethiopian would understand such patriarchal paternalism, and it was also the truth. Legesse said he would phone the supervisor.

Arlene needed to be gone, but she couldn't leave without the proper governmental paperwork, and the wheels of bureaucracy were grinding ever so slowly.

*January 13, 1977, Thursday (first recorded on November 13, 1975)*

*The sacrifice of thanksgiving gladdens my heart. When you come into My Presence, let it be in a spirit of praise. When you make a fresh vow of commitment to Me each morning, let it be in a spirit of praise and thanksgiving—not in heaviness, as if it were a burdensome duty to offer your life afresh to Me. Let it be in the spirit of My servant Isaiah, "Here am I. Send me." Let me touch your lips each morning with a burning coal. Let me anoint you each day with my Spirit of gladness.*

## Questions for Reflection/Discussion

1. The ancient concept of "anointing" was a physical action, such as the rubbing of oil on the head to symbolize the presence of God. When have you experienced physical anointing of some kind?

2. What is one of your favorite songs to evoke the true meaning of Christmas?

3. To whom do you go to confess your sins and be held accountable?

# Message 76

Let all bitterness, and wrath, and anger, and clamour, and evil speaking, be put away from you, with all malice: and be ye kind one to another, tenderhearted, forgiving one another, even as God for Christ's sake hath forgiven you.

Ephesians 4:31–32 (KJV)

If she couldn't get out of the country, she could at least get out of the house—away from the mess, the clang of the phone, and the knock on the door. Arlene and her friend Rachel had been invited to a small dinner at SIM headquarters. It was a lovely time, and Arlene reported that, at least for those few hours, the joy of the Lord returned to her.

*January 14, 1977, Friday*

*There are many evils besetting the world for the devil is trying to make the most of the remaining time. He is deceiving even leaders in the Church with his subtle heresies so that humans try to usurp the prerogatives of God. The lawlessness of Satan is being evidenced in every area of life. It behooves you to walk more carefully. Pray to be shown how to use your time wisely. Pray to be in My <u>highest</u> will at all times. The good is not enough. It must be the <u>best</u> use of your talents, resources, and time in these difficult last days.*

## ✚ Questions for Reflection/Discussion

1. "Clamour" is an interesting word. Other translations use "outcry," "harsh words," and "shouting." Where do you hear clamoring in your life? Are you willing for it to be "put away from you" and embrace kindness as an alternative?

2. Arlene and Rachel managed to get away for a few hours, which restored her joy. What do you do to "get away"?

3. What did the Lord tell Arlene was not enough?

# Message 77

But rejoice in so far as you share Christ's sufferings, that you may also rejoice and be glad when His glory is revealed.

1 Peter 4:13 (RSV)

When Arlene left the farm for the South Sudan in 1954, she traveled with her brand-new Argos C3 camera. Twenty-three years of ministry later, she had traded the South Sudan for Ethiopia and her old Argos for a Minolta. It was time to transition again, so with her Ethiopia departure date finally set for the end of January, her Minolta was one of the last things to sell.

*January 17, 1977, Monday*

> *Suffering has come upon you, My child, but it is only to prove your faith in Me. Hold fast to My Truth and you shall not be dismayed when others desert or reproach you for My sake. Remain steadfast in prayer and I shall overcome this evil assault of the enemy. Continue to glorify Me in praise and I* <u>shall</u> <u>restore</u> <u>this</u> <u>situation</u>. *My Power shall be resting upon you when it is needed. Go in faith, doubting nothing, when I call you to go in My Name. Fear not the interference of the enemy. I shall vindicate My Plan. I shall be glorified in this problem.*

## Questions for Reflection/Discussion

1. Have you ever had to leave something behind when you moved?

2. Have you ever been left behind or deserted?

3. Messages 77 and 78 each contain benedictions: "Go in faith, doubting nothing" and "Go in peace." What is a benediction/blessing that you find especially meaningful and why?

# ✚ Message 78

"Behold, God is my salvation;
    I will trust, and will not be afraid;
for the LORD GOD is my strength and my song,
    and he has become my salvation."

With joy you will draw water from the wells of salvation.
And you will say in that day:

"Give thanks to the LORD,
    call upon his name;
make known his deeds among the nations,
    proclaim that his name is exalted.

"Sing praises to the LORD, for he has done gloriously;
    let this be known in all the earth."

                                        Isaiah 12:2–5 (RSV)

Arlene's final journal pages written in Addis Ababa itemized friend after friend coming to bless her. Marian, who would be staying on the African continent, flew to Addis to stay overnight with Arlene once more, taking supper by the fireplace, talking into the wee hours.

The struggle with Legesse continued, including a rancorous phone call in which he quoted Lamentations to her: "Thou hast made us offscouring and refuse among the peoples." After the call, Arlene paced the floor of her bedroom until 2:00 a.m. when the anointing love of Jesus returned to her. After that, she was able to sleep. She began the next day with a song on her lips:

*I am not skilled to understand*
*What God has willed, what God has planned.*
*I only know at his right hand*
*Stands one who is my Savior.*

She listed Scripture after Scripture in her journal and prayed in tongues for a long time. Then she wrote, *Help Legesse to give me up as a sacrifice of love for You, Jesus.* She eventually shared that prayer with him, and he agreed to make it his own.

Near the end of January, her mission supervisor invited a large group of friends to his home for a goodbye dinner for her. He read from the book of Job: "When he has tried me, I shall come forth as gold." Then they gave Arlene the gift of a gold Lalibela cross. She wrote in her journal that her sorrow was at last turning into peace.

Her final Ethiopian message from the Lord arrived as a benediction to her decade of sojourning in that ancient land.

*January 29, 1977, Saturday*

> *Yes, I am the God of your salvation and with joy you will draw water from the wells. You will call upon My Name in praise and thanksgiving for I have forgiven your sin. You will prophesy to My glory among the nations and wherever I call you to follow Me, you will go in My Strength and My Joy. You will trust and not fear what anyone can say or do. You have humbled yourself before Me, and I shall comfort you. Go in peace.*

## ✚ Questions for Reflection/Discussion

1. Isaiah says, "Make known his deeds among the nations." What five miracle stories from the Bible do you know?

2. What friend of yours would travel a long way to say goodbye in person if you were moving out of the country?

3. What are you especially thankful to God for today?

## ✚ Message 79

Daleth. Geslacht aan geslacht zal Uw werken roemen; en zij zullen Uw mogendheden verkondigen.

Psalm 145:4 (Dutch)

Back home in Sioux Center, Iowa, Arlene was on furlough. She was living with Ma and Grada in the Second Avenue home her parents had built before Pa's sudden death by heart failure. She was glad to be helping care for Ma who, due to her forgetfulness, required regular attentiveness, even though she didn't always know who Arlene was.

Arlene received speaking requests, but it wasn't yet time for that. She tried to catch up on correspondence, but concern for Ma made concentration on any task difficult. And then there was the steady flow of visitors reestablishing relationships now that Arlene was home.

She spent a lot of time repressing the grief and anxiety that poured out in tears when she was finally alone. She prayed,

*God, this waiting and isolation in my own home is hard. Please help me as I pass through these dark days of trial. Give me a thankful heart.*

One morning in early April, the anointing love of Jesus returned. A week later, she wrote again, *4:00 a.m. Jesus anointed me!* The next day she prayed,

*Forgive me, Jesus, I do <u>trust</u> You. I've allowed doubts and fears concerning the future to enter so often.*

She sometimes recited or read psalms in Dutch to her mother. One day, the psalm was 145, including the potent verse 4, "One generation shall laud thy works to another, and shall declare thy mighty acts." She wrote, *Reading Psalm 145 to Mom—Wow.* She also copied into her journal Hebrews 13:8 (RSV): *Jesus Christ is the same yesterday and today and for ever.* That day, for the first time since Ethiopia, she rerecorded a message from the Lord.

*April 19, 1977, Tuesday (first recorded on February 4, 1976)*

> *Do you believe that I am the same—in all your yesterdays? I have loved you when you were rejected by others, guided you when you were confused by others. My Love for you is constant, unchanging, unconditional. I am with you <u>now</u> in this disheartening situation. Claim My Power to rule in it—to overrule the enemy who is trying to distract your gaze from Me, I shall be with you in all your tomorrows. Trust in Me <u>NOW</u>.*

## ✚ Questions for Reflection/Discussion

1. Where is "home" to you? Why?

2. Who will care for you in your old age?

3. What's a song you sing about heaven?

# ✛ Message 80

I am my beloved's and I am the one he desires.
Song of Solomon 7:10 (TLB)

Maurie Te Paske was born in Sioux Center, Iowa, on January 5, 1916. By the time he was twenty-two, he had earned his law degree from the University of Iowa. He returned to his home town to practice law, and two years later, he was elected the youngest mayor in his home state, a position he held for thirty-four years when he decided not to run for re-election at the age of fifty-eight. Two years later, on July 13, 1976, he was driving his car through Iowa's capital city when he pulled to the curb, slumped against the steering wheel, and died of a heart attack.

Arlene was in Addis Ababa when she learned of Maurie's death. He and his family had factored large in Arlene's own journey. Maurie's mother, Agnes, was the Sunday school teacher who taught Arlene to sing "Jesus Loves Me," and Maurie was serving on the Reformed Church Board of Foreign Missions when Arlene left for the South Sudan in 1955. He represented the board at her commissioning service. Today in Sioux Center, she wrote in her journal,

> A year ago that Maurie Te Paske died. And I constantly go back in my thoughts to what was happening in Addis a year ago— busy with curriculum revision—Legesse becoming friendly. Very happy days usually.

The Lord whispered a cautionary nudge.

*July 13, 1977, Wednesday*

> The Cross in your life can be a rich gateway to My treasures if you will allow Me to do a _deep_ work in your heart. You have received My baptism in the Holy Spirit but you are not allowing Me to minister freely through you. You are claiming

*only a superficial baptism—looking too much at signs and feelings. When you let Me do a deep cleansing of the past, more of My Power will flow through you.*

## ✚ Questions for Reflection/Discussion

1. What are some songs you learned as a child? Do any of them continue to feed your spirit today?

2. Who is a leader you remember from your hometown or church? What about them served as an example to you?

3. What do you suppose Message 80 means by "a deep cleansing of the past"?

# ✚ *Message 81*

"Be still, and know that I am God.
    I am exalted among the nations,
    I am exalted in the earth!"

Psalm 46:10 (RSV)

For seven weeks that autumn, Arlene went out on "deputation." This meant that she represented her denomination's foreign mission activities by reporting back to the churches who had supported her through their donations and prayers. Her denomination scheduled her to speak, show slides, and answer questions. She spoke at a wide range of locations, from living rooms to church sanctuaries for various age groups and numbers of people. In her journal, she recorded another prayer:

> *Jesus, I invite You to come sit with me where I am now—to enter into all that is happening concerning this deputation trip—concerning what's happening to my Ethiopian family—concerning the working out of your plan for me. You are the Good Shepherd, my Guide. I want to be a conqueror, an overcomer. Maybe I don't know what this involves or what I'm asking You, but You know all things. You know that I love You.*

Deputation was more of a responsibility than a delight to her. She was a trained and experienced nurse, comfortable in front of the classroom. She was also a mature woman of faith, glad to lead a Bible study or prayer meeting. But public speaking was another matter, requiring nimble adjustments to new audiences—many of whom had heard stories of miracles, demons, and the work of the Holy Spirit on the African continent. Of these people, some were set to question the veracity of her own experience and very few would have been truly comfortable at her Mettu church. She wrote in her journal:

*Meeting at Presb church at night where I showed slides and answered questions. Then tea and all the noise of many voices. This still is the most tiring of all to me. If I could just be whisked home after speaking.*

Arlene poured out her heart when she spoke about her Mettu church, while at the same time doubting she'd ever be able to return there. She knew that the Mettu church had been closed for a time and that many leaders had been imprisoned. Now she heard they were holding services again, but she knew she couldn't consider returning to Ethiopia unless they invited her. She was a potential danger to her Ethiopian community because of continuing antagonisms between the revolutionary government and the United States.

Just before Thanksgiving week, she arrived home from the whirlwind days of deputation. She took her place in caring for Ma and tending to household chores, such as telephoning the plumber to come and fix the toilet. Then, for the first time since summer, she received a message from the Lord.

*November 22, 1977, Tuesday*

*"Be still and know that I am God"—and take hold of My Peace within you. Take hold of My Love within you—My Power to guide and strengthen you and sustain you. In quiet, confident trust you will find My strength for this day.*

## ✠ Questions for Reflection/Discussion

1. When are you "still"?

2. What responsibilities do you have that exhaust you?

3. In her prayer, Arlene traveled through her imagination to her supporting churches, to Ethiopia, and to her future. In your prayer today, where are you traveling?

## ✚ *Message 82*

"You did not choose me, but I chose you and appointed you that you should go and bear fruit and that your fruit should abide; so that whatever you ask the Father in my name, he may give it to you."
John 15:16 (RSV)

Arlene's season of furlough was nearing an end, and she would no longer be paid unless she accepted a new call to the mission field. She had hoped to return to Ethiopia, but that didn't seem feasible. She needed to resume work for financial reasons as well as keeping up her skills and knowledge in her medical field. There were options locally, but she had also received an invitation to work and teach at her alma mater, the Frontier Nursing University in Kentucky. Since this latter option offered her welcome flexibility in case an overseas position opened up, she applied for a nursing and midwifery licensure in Kentucky and then prayed,

*God are you leading me out of this wilderness journey? I believe that all things are working together for good to those who love You. Triune God, I love You.*

The next day, she received this message.

*December 2, 1977, Friday*

*I have called you into a ministry of fruit-bearing, and you have accepted this appointment. In My Name go, knowing that what you ask in My nature of Love will be given you. Asking in My Name means asking those things that are within My Nature. I have commanded you to love, so be guided by My Love. Ask in faith. Standing on My Words (for they will help you), now hold fast against doubts and fears. Ask much—but always in My Nature of Love.*

## ✚ Questions for Reflection/Discussion

1. What season of your life (whether long or short) felt like the wanderings of the children of Israel in their "wilderness journey"?

2. When was a time that you sensed God choosing something for you even before anyone else chose you?

3. How do you see God at work in the missionaries your church supports?

# ✚ *Message 83*

How precious it is, Lord, to realize that you are thinking about me constantly! I can't even count how many times a day your thoughts turn toward me. And when I waken in the morning, you are still thinking of me!

Psalm 139:17–18 (TLB)

After speaking in many different places across North America, Arlene was due to speak in the morning services at her own home church. She felt as if she had saved the worst for last. The Wednesday prior to the service, she wrote,

> *Mom is restless . . . and I feel like I was able to accomplish nothing. Speaking Sunday weighs heavy on me. Why is this required of me when I find it SO difficult? Haven't had time to put it together at all. I'm not strong enuf emotionally yet.*

On Friday, she went to a nearby park just to get away, pray, and journal.

> *Can't get Sunday's message together. Headache.*

On Saturday, she was busy all morning doing house duties and caring for her mother. But later that day, she received this message, indicating that God had already moved beyond Sunday.

*December 17, 1977, Saturday*

> *I have a purpose for you that is beyond your understanding or your natural talents. I will open up the way when the time is ripe. You have been straining too hard, trying to accomplish too much. Your striving is futile. It is the enemy's way. My prophecy for you is for the distant future. You will be ready for it to be fulfilled in you only if you let Me choose the pattern for each of your days. I am quietly preparing you for this new work*

*of healing. As your own memories of the painful past are being
healed, you are growing toward this ministry. I am leading the
way. Trust in Me!*

## ✛ Questions for Reflection/Discussion

1. What is your relationship with deadlines? How are they
   helpful, and how are they maddening to you?

2. Jesus said that prophets are honored everywhere except
   in their own hometown. How would you feel if given the
   opportunity to speak at your home church?

3. What have you prayed for although you had no idea how
   God would bring it to pass? How did it work out for you?

# ✚ Message 84

For my thoughts are not your thoughts,
    neither are your ways my ways, says the LORD.
For as the heavens are higher than the earth,
    so are my ways higher than your ways
    and my thoughts than your thoughts.

                                    Isaiah 55:8–9 (RSV)

Arlene didn't report the results of that Sunday at her church. Her unusually brief journal entry looked like one from her first *Five Year Diary* that she received on her nineteenth birthday:

> *Up at 5:30. Went over message twice. Brkf. 8:45 service and 11:00 with Rev. Rezelman in charge. To Gert for dinner. Home in P.M. To Bernice and Howard for supper. I stayed home with Mom at night.*

Like last Saturday's whisper from the Lord, she was moving on.

*December 19, 1977, Monday (first recorded on August 1, 1976)*

> *My ways are higher than your ways. When you cannot see the reason, trust Me to make it clear in My own way and time. I know your <u>deepest</u> needs, not just your superficial needs. I am changing your circumstances and attitudes as fast as you will let Me. Lift this disappointment and leave it with Me. When I close a door it is because I will open a better one—when you are ready. Let Me use this frustration. Let Me take the sting out of it. Bask in My Love for you—not the love of others. My Love changes not!*

## ✚ *Questions for Reflection/Discussion*

1. What's a practice you started years ago and are still doing today?

2. Do you recall hearing a missionary speak when you were a child? How would you describe the impact it had on you?

3. Imagine that you were Arlene's mother. What might you have felt or thought the day your daughter spoke at church?

# 1978
## January 29 to March 9

off the snow and ice again - Still 10-20°.
I bought meat and prepared supper for
Dr. Gilbert, Molly, Ruth B. in Molly's Apt.
Wrote 7 letters and went to bed at 10³⁹

January 29, 1978 Sunday.
    Up at 7¹⁵ thinking I was late for going
to work but it's Sunday _ my favorite day.
Light snow _

    "Jesus said to him, "No one who puts his
hand to the plow and looks back is fit for the
kingdom of God." Luke 9:62 _

Prophecy = "When I call you, you must not look back.
You have put your hand to the plow and there is
much, work to be done - There is no turning back
for those who commit their lives to bringing in My
Kingdom - No excuses, no procrastinations are now
valid. You cannot stand still any longer. You
must go forward - Follow Me."

    Three weeks in Hyden now:
    1) feel this was a step directed of the Lord.
    2) God arranged for Bernedette to orient me _
    3) Winter _ and enjoying it _ exercise is good _
    4) Quiet privacy to think and pray _
    5) Beautiful view of sunrise over mts _
    6) Presb. Church & RevHood + Bible Study _
    7)

# ✚ *Message 85*

> As they were going along the road, a man said to him, "I will follow you wherever you go." And Jesus said to him, "Foxes have holes, and birds of the air have nests; but the Son of man has nowhere to lay his head." To another he said, "Follow me." But he said, "Lord, let me first go and bury my father." But he said to him, "Leave the dead to bury their own dead; but as for you, go and proclaim the kingdom of God." Another said, "I will follow you, Lord; but let me first say farewell to those at my home." Jesus said to him, "No one who puts his hand to the plow and looks back is fit for the kingdom of God."
>
> Luke 9:57–62 (RSV)

Arlene had been at Frontier Nursing in Hyden, Kentucky, for three weeks. She was living in an apartment on campus, serving as a nurse in the new hospital, and going to classes, learning new technologies and medical practices that would serve her when she returned to the mission field.

Although Ethiopia was completely closed to her now, possibilities were emerging on the African continent in Egypt and Zambia.

*January 29, 1978, Sunday*

> *When I call you, you must not look back. You have put your hand to the plow and there is much work to be done. There is no turning back for those who commit their lives to bringing in My Kingdom. No excuses, no procrastinations are now valid. You cannot stand still any longer. You must go forward. Follow Me.*

✠ *Questions for Reflection/Discussion*

1. Why would it be bad for the farmer to put a hand to the plow and look back?

2. Message 85 told Arlene that she could no longer stand still. What do you think she was waiting for?

3. Is there an area of your life in which God is telling you to stop waiting?

# ✠ *Message 86*

And my God will supply every need of yours according to his riches in glory in Christ Jesus.

Philippians 4:19 (RSV)

Arlene went to visit her pastor. For an hour and a half, she told him about the past two years. He listened carefully and offered the following suggestions and questions, which she recorded:

1. *You are in a grieving time.*

2. *You have been uprooted.*

3. *Do you have any resentments? (She recorded that she couldn't think of any.)*

4. *You have an accumulation of exhaustion which may require many weeks of rest.*

5. *While you wait for God's next calling, you should get established in one place, but not one as strenuous as the Frontier Nursing job with its twenty-four hour on-call demands.*

*March 2, 1978, Thursday (first recorded on August 29, 1975)*

*When you become tense, rest in Me at once. Do not dally with any thoughts of weariness or self-pity. Do not criticize others or become impatient with them. Ask for and claim My patience— My supply for all your needs. I am concerned with all the details of your life. You need not be anxious if you stop at once to open the window of your spirit to the flooding of My Love.*

## ✚ Questions for Reflection/Discussion

1. Is there someone you personally know who is wealthy enough to supply your every need according to their riches? What's the difference between their wealth and "riches in glory in Christ Jesus"?

2. What do you find especially valuable about Arlene's pastor's counsel?

3. Why do you suppose Arlene chose to revisit this particular message two and a half years later?

# ✚ *Message 87*

Now the rabble that was among them had a strong craving; and the people of Israel also wept again, and said, "O that we had meat to eat! We remember the fish we ate in Egypt for nothing, the cucumbers, the melons, the leeks, the onions, and the garlic; but now our strength is dried up, and there is nothing at all but this manna to look at."

Now the manna was like coriander seed, and its appearance like that of bdellium. The people went about and gathered it, and ground it in mills or beat it in mortars, and boiled it in pots, and made cakes of it; and the taste of it was like the taste of cakes baked with oil. When the dew fell upon the camp in the night, the manna fell with it.

Numbers 11:4–9 (RSV)

"Come to me, all who labor and are heavy laden, and I will give you rest. Take my yoke upon you, and learn from me; for I am gentle and lowly in heart, and you will find rest for your souls. For my yoke is easy, and my burden is light."

Matthew 11:28–30 (RSV)

Arlene assisted a student in the labor ward, resulting in the delivery of a living female. All was well, and the student was especially glad because it was her tenth delivery, which fulfilled her midwifery graduation requirement.

The next morning, as a dense, dark fog settled onto the town, Arlene wrote, *God is a Light within me and joy rises.* She read from the book of Numbers and then prayed,

*Just what I needed. What a feast. Thank you, Jesus. You are the Bread of Life. Now I see myself as a pilgrim on this wilderness journey toward heaven, but not a wanderer. Praise the Lord. The Cloud moves from time to time. But the Manna, His Word, sustains me. Praise the Lord.*

She was in her small apartment that had been renovated out of the old horse barn. Later in the day, she would drive into Hazard for the first time in over two months. But first, she recorded this message.

*March 9, 1978, Thursday*

> *You are not tired today because My Love has renewed your energies. This is the secret—to rest in Me for a few minutes between your tasks. Let Me renew your strength as you look to Me. Hand over your burdens to Me often throughout each day. <u>Let no fearful or critical thought double the load</u>. <u>My Love is an enabling Power</u> that will carry you through pressures without strain. Come to Me when you are weary and let Me refresh you.*

## ✚ Questions for *Reflection/Discussion*

1. Has there ever been a time when you were tired of the food you were eating? When you needed some variety in your diet?

2. What's the distinction Arlene drew between a pilgrim and a wanderer? What was the destination of Arlene's pilgrimage?

3. What does Message 87 say that "fearful or critical thought" will result in? Conversely, what is the antidote to weariness?

# ✚ *Message 88*

Fear not, for I am with you. Do not be dismayed. I am your God. I will strengthen you; I will help you; I will uphold you with my victorious right hand.

I am holding you by your right hand—I, the Lord your God—and I say to you, Don't be afraid; I am here to help you.

Isaiah 41:10, 13 (TLB)

On Monday, Arlene was midwife for a breech delivery that took all day. She was bone-weary when the director of nursing asked if she would agree to continue in the ward for the next two months. She was too tired to even think about it. She was grateful she didn't have to work until evening and wrote, *I need time with My Lord.*

*March 21, 1978, Tuesday (first recorded on September 1, 1975)*

*My child, I have loved you with an everlasting Love, and I have appointed you to bear much fruit. Fear not to go forth and do the works I have called you to do. The enemy has assaulted you, but you have nothing to fear. My rod and My staff strengthen you. I shall spread a table before you in the presence of your enemies. Your cup shall run over with My Joy. Goodness and mercy shall flow out of you, and you shall dwell in My Presence all the days of your life.*

## ✚ *Questions for Reflection/Discussion*

1. A major theme of the Lord's messages to Arlene has been fear. How did the Lord counsel her to deal with fear?

2. According to Message 88, what did the Lord appoint Arlene to do?

3. The second half of this message is based on Psalm 23, but what is the subtle difference between the message and the psalm?

 *Message 89*

He has delivered us from the dominion of darkness and transferred us to the kingdom of his beloved Son.

Colossians 1:13 (RSV)

In the month of March, Arlene disregarded her pastor's counsel that she get some rest, as evidenced by her journal entries during this time:

*Very tired.*
*Too weary to think tonight.*
*I am so tired.*

The entire rural countryside was tired. She took her life in her hands just driving into town to get gas because the mountain road was falling apart. She walked to church for Bible study, but the electricity went out.

Connection with the world outside of the Kentucky mountains was sometimes difficult. While considering a return to Africa, valuable information she requested kept getting lost in the mail—which prompted her mission supervisor to write,

*Strange to realize how isolated one can be in the middle of a country that boasts of its transportation and communications.*

Arlene's faith practices continued, including walking through the forest to the prayer rock that had long been a sacred place for her. It was upon this very rock that she had laid face down in 1959 after hearing that her father had suffered a heart attack. Now she went to the rock and as she grew quiet in God's presence, his whisper returned.

*March 23, 1978, Thursday*

> *When a spirit of deep weariness comes upon you, know that it is not from Me but from the enemy. Take dominion over this spirit in My Power and cast it out quickly. You need not allow the enemy to oppress you. With your first awakening thought each morning, claim a circle of My purifying fire around you.*

Arlene was indeed called back to the African continent—to Zambia—initially as principal tutor of an established nursing school in Katete and eventually to Macha. She traveled from Hyden, Kentucky, to Sioux Center at the end of June and left for Zambia in mid-August.

As she prepared to leave, she wrote down this prayer, including 2 Samuel 7:25 (TLB):

> *Mom is resting on the davenport. I also commit her to You— and all the others in our family. May we __ALL__ meet again. "And now, Lord God, __do__ as you have promised concerning me and my family."*

## ✚ Questions for Reflection/Discussion

1. Do you have a place that is your private chapel, like Arlene's prayer rock? If not, do you see the value of finding or creating such a space?

2. Do you have a pattern of a "first awakening thought" each morning?

3. Why was Arlene's family as close-knit as it seems to have been?

 *Zambia*

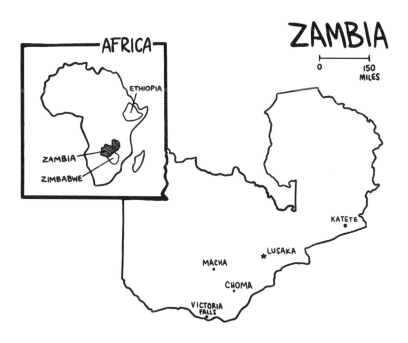

AFRICA

ETHIOPIA

ZAMBIA

ZIMBABWE

ZAMBIA

0    150 MILES

KATETE

LUSAKA

MACHA

CHOMA

VICTORIA FALLS

# 1979
## April 11

Worked on June Schedule in H.M. Also Barbara Williams and ――――― two nurses from Copperbelt came to see St Francis c̄ the thought of working here. They visited school at 12³⁰.

Mtg c̄ Cairns, Matron + Kathleen at 2 P.M. Working out details about Graduation - etc. Also Cairns wants me to be on committee c̄ him and matron to decide what to do about ZAMBIAN Violet's assault on Kathleen - midwifery tutor. I tried to get excused but Cairns insisted. This could have all kinds of political as well as other ramifications since Violet's husband Benedict Zulu is a party member. We are to meet Thurs at 2 P.M. and hear stories of all those involved.

Trying to get stains out of material for living room drapes. Looks like tea c̄ sugar stains. April 11, 1979 Wednesday

✳ "Because you have remained faithful to Me in love, I will deliver you from this attack of the enemy, He has no power over those who call upon

# ✚ *Message 90*

Then, after doing all those things,
    I will pour out my Spirit upon all people.
Your sons and daughters will prophesy.
    Your old men will dream dreams,
    and your young men will see visions.
In those days I will pour out my Spirit
    even on servants—men and women alike.
And I will cause wonders in the heavens and on the earth—
    blood and fire and columns of smoke.
The sun will become dark,
    and the moon will turn blood red
    before that great and terrible day of the LORD arrives.
But everyone who calls on the name of the LORD
    will be saved.

Joel 2:28–32a (NLT)

Violet was a nursing student who graduated and began her midwifery residency at the hospital where Arlene served, and Kathleen was a new midwife tutor from England. When some conflict arose between the two, Violet lashed out and Kathleen brought her grievance to Arlene, threatening to leave immediately. Arlene asked Kathleen to at least wait until the hospital administrator, Dr. Cairns, returned from a trip.

Arlene didn't want to add the general question of hospital personnel to her workload, but the hospital and school were intertwined since students received practical education by putting in hours at the hospital—the scheduling of which was a primary headache for Arlene. She concluded one day's entry by writing,

*Back to the office after supper, correcting exams until 10 P.M. Put in a 14 hour day.*

She wasn't on call for labor and delivery, but she struggled with a wearisome workload, having traded in the joys of witnessing new birth for the stresses of school administration.

During Holy Week, Dr. Cairns returned and appointed Arlene to a three-person panel to adjudicate the altercation between Violet and Kathleen. Arlene begged off. She was concerned about the complexity of the case since it situated an instructor against a student, someone new to the community against someone well-established, and a European against a Zambian. Further complications arose because Violet's husband was a regional politician. Dr. Cairns wouldn't release Arlene from the panel and set the hearing for Maundy Thursday.

On Wednesday morning, Arlene received assurance from the Lord.

*April 11, 1979, Wednesday*

> *Because you have remained faithful to Me in love, I will deliver you from this attack of the enemy. He has no power over those who call upon the protection of My Name. I will rescue you and guide you out of this difficulty, for you have called upon Me in faith. Your adversaries will have no power over you. You will trample underfoot Satan's efforts to distract you. Victory will be Mine in your life.*

The hearing was held. Violet was given a three-month suspension but allowed to continue, which satisfied Kathleen enough to remain. Although the immediate crisis had been averted, there would be trouble during Arlene's final decade in Africa—demons, medicines, diseases, water, war, crime, economics, and more!

Throughout her life, Arlene would continue to write letters, prayers, and almost daily journal entries. But her season of written messages from the Lord now ceased.

## Questions for Reflection/Discussion

1. In what ways do you hope to imitate Arlene's faith journey?

2. Have you accepted the invitation from Jesus to follow him?

3. How would you articulate your own mission?

# ✚ *Acknowledgments*

Arlene Schuiteman, who is turning ninety-nine as this book is released, has placed her lifetime of journals and letters into my care. They will eventually find their way to the Joint Archives of Holland which is located in Holland, Michigan (https://hope.edu/library/joint-archives-holland/).

Arlene and her sister Grada Kiel have been participants in this project from its inception, and it could not have happened without them. Karissa Meier, my student assistant at Northwestern College, combed through Arlene's journals to ensure that I did not overlook any of the personal prophecies transcribed there. Karissa's fellow students in the theatre ensemble she was a part of graciously listened to readings of some of the first prophecies we found. They insisted that we should find and share them all. Others who read advance editions of this book and for whom I'm deeply grateful are Hannah Nickolay, Joseph Barker, Ed Gillette, Juliana Else, Doris Bohm, and Julie Gillette.

Over a period of several years, Patricia Anders edited the entire series of Arlene Schuiteman books. She has been as careful and encouraging as any author could hope. For this book, Kristin Brouwer, Kate Walker, and Sarah Welch provided valuable input on the reflection questions, Phil Frank typeset the book, and Bradford Rusick designed the cover. I'm also grateful to Katherine Lempares for creating the artistic renderings of the African continent, and to Daniel Barker, who took the photo of Arlene and me (see the next page).

My pastors Jon Opgenorth and Brian Keepers, along with Trinity Reformed Church (Orange City, Iowa), have shepherded my work over the years. May every artist have such a community! Thanks especially to Anne Mead and Anita Cirulis for praying. Finally, this project owes every step in its journey to my beloved Karen Bohm Barker.

Arlene and Jeff Barker at Arlene's home in Sioux Center, Iowa (2017).